Praise for

UNEXPECTED CONNECTIONS

"If you really want to gain insight, you have to roll up your sleeves, get down in the trenches, and experience life with people. Matt Peacock has invested years gaining that insight and shares with us the critical need to address social isolation in our ministries of help and healing. This book helps you learn how relationships and connections unlock the potential to elevate people as we bring them into the Kingdom of God. Compassionate churches and faithful nonprofits can forge amazing partnerships as they engage people in the mission of Jesus. The vision and practical tools to accomplish that goal are found in Unexpected Connections!"

—TIM HAWKS

Lead Pastor, Hill Country Bible Church (Austin, Texas)

"If you are looking for a book to challenge you, your church or nonprofit to courageously look through a new lens about impacting the world with the Kingdom of God, Unexpected Connections is for you! This book introduces you to a collaborative, long-term strategy of connecting to people, especially those in social isolation. It's a Biblical, Kingdom-oriented guide for those who are ready to get serious about being the body of Christ on earth. It is easy to read, profound in its concepts, and well worth the time!"

—TRAVIS G. BUNDRICK

Director, Strategic Church Solutions (Georgetown, Texas)

"Read this book if you want to see love break out in your community in practical and lasting ways. Matt is not writing down a theory he wonders about; he is writing from real work that has delivered genuine results. Unexpected Connections can help you learn how to transform your community, your church, and yourself."

—SCOTT HEARE

Senior Pastor, Lake Travis United Methodist Church (Austin, Texas)

"In Unexpected Connections, Matt describes the beauty of synergistic relationships in ministering to the community. Lake Travis Crisis Ministries has worked with Matt and the Partners in Hope team for many years now, and we've witnessed God changing the lives of people who would not have been reached without his unique approach. This book tells that story in a powerful way, and I definitely recommend it."

—PAM WOLFE

Board President, Lake Travis Crisis Ministries (Austin, Texas)

"Through real-life examples of jumping deep into ministry in his community, Matt Peacock weaves together a concise 'Kingdom Serving Paradigm' that invites us into a new way of moving people living in social isolation into community. The book is full of key examples and tools for how to get started in building Kingdom partnerships. I highly recommend this book as an essential read for any church or nonprofit leader looking for better ways to reach the lost and hurting in their community!"

—MICHELLE BRIGANCE

Missions Pastor, Austin Christian Fellowship (Austin, Texas)

"What a compelling story—and filled with so much practical insight. Unexpected Connections is a must-read for churches!"

—RICHARD VER STEEG
Former Church Elder, The Lakeway Church (Lakeway, Texas)

"Unexpected Connections is an excellent book about social isolation, church member training, and the importance of partnering with any and all community groups for maximum Kingdom impact. Each of the small revelations Matt describes are actually HUGE."

—TRACI RHOADES
Ministry Leader, Author & Blogger (Grand Rapids, Michigan)

"As I read Matt's book, not only was I inspired by the insights God had given him, but I was also deeply challenged by the practical way Matt and his nonprofit ministry demonstrated the love of God to their 'Jerusalem,' Lake Travis. This book is well worth the read."

—MIKE BOOTH
Pastor, Rizen Fellowship (Moore, Oklahoma)

UNEXPECTED
CONNECTIONS

How God is rewiring a community to
fight social isolation and grow the Kingdom

———— ✦ ————

MATT PEACOCK

IRIDESCENT PRESS
Austin, Texas

Unexpected Connections
How God is rewiring a community to fight social isolation and grow the Kingdom

Published by:
IRIDESCENT PRESS
15104 N. Flamingo Drive
Austin, Texas 78734

All of the people described in this book are real, but their names have been changed to provide anonymity.

Printed in the United States of America.

Concept Development & Research: Kenny Camp (www.KennethACamp.com)
Developmental Editing & Content: Susan Priddy (www.SusanPriddy.com)
Cover Design & Interior Layout: Kendra Cagle (www.5LakesDesign.com)

Library of Congress Control Number: 2020911697

ISBN: 978-1-7352717-0-5 (hardcover)
         978-1-7352717-1-2 (paperback)
         978-1-7352717-2-9 (Kindle)
         978-1-7352717-3-6 (ePub)

Matt Peacock
www.PartnersInHopeLakeTravis.org
PartnersInHopeLakeTravis@gmail.com

DEDICATION

This book is dedicated to my family.

To my wife Cynthia who has been my life partner and ministry partner since 1993. Nothing I've done could have been done without you. You've been the backbone of our home and life together. Thank you for your constant support that allowed us to pursue these opportunities to serve others.

To my kids Nathan and Kennan who were flexible when ministry took us to new cities. With each move, you left friends and familiarities behind for a new place, new people, a new start. Thank you for your sacrifices, and I pray that God will use all of these experiences in meaningful ways in your lives.

To my Mom and my late Father who prayed for me my whole life. You showed me what loving other people looked like, even before I understood that's what you did. Thank you for all your faithful prayers for me and my family.

In my life, each one of you is
a true blessing from God.

TABLE OF CONTENTS

ACKNOWLEDGEMENTS

*I'd like to express my sincere thanks
to the following people:*

To Kenny Camp who worked with me to launch Partners in Hope and start this book, as well as for encouraging me as a friend throughout the process.

To Susan Priddy who worked diligently to assemble all my thoughts and create this book, as well as doing all it takes to actually put the book into readers' hands.

To Brian Smith who challenged me to see the applications for this book and provided the resources to make it happen.

To the launch team at The Church at Bee Cave who made the ministry vision become reality by stepping into the unknown and sharing Christ's love with the community.

To the many Board Members of Partners in Hope who supported the vision and demonstrated servant leadership with their active involvement.

To the staff members of Partners in Hope, including Diahn (Dee) Ehlers and Denise Ray, who have poured themselves into this ministry, loving people and giving their talents to build what I never could have by myself.

To all of the community volunteers who served with us and represented us well—especially John Alger, David Schaerdel, Bo Guevara and Jim Schaeffer who served many a hot day with skill and heart.

To Austin Christian Fellowship for believing in this ministry as a foundational supporter, investing in us and equipping us as an organization.

To the hundreds of donors who trusted us with resources they could have sent somewhere else but, instead, used their gifts to make an impact on local families by supporting me and our team.

To Mike Booth who took the time to mentor me as a new believer and showed me what walking with someone looks like.

To the Lord who has shown grace, patience and love for me all these years. Thank you for putting so many incredible people in my life, for picking me up when I fail, and for putting me out there again in the midst of the incredible things you do. Every day I'm grateful for the opportunities to be part of your work.

FOREWORD
BY DR. PETE DEISON

———— ✦ ————

As someone who's been in ministry for more than 50 years, I am genuinely inspired by the principles Matt shares through this insightful book.

In *Unexpected Connections*, Matt describes in great detail how he and his team are fighting the epidemic of social isolation while transforming the way communities serve their neighbors in need. He not only shines a light on an emerging ministry opportunity, but he also gives us a unique formula for taking advantage of it. His moving stories and specific examples demonstrate how those of us in ministry can follow his lead in bringing the Gospel to life on a daily basis.

I've had the honor of knowing Matt for his entire life, and it's obvious to me why God chose him to write this book. He has been in the trenches with all aspects of ministry for decades, and he's been a loyal servant—even when the Lord took him down roads he never would have chosen himself. I'm pretty sure his natural instinct was to avoid some of those detours, but his faith kept him firmly on track.

Matt has a rare ability to balance leadership, vision and focus with compassion, authenticity and patience. Loving perseverance is simply part of his DNA, and he is solid as a rock. No matter what obstacles he encounters, he never lets the process obscure the value of the people he's committed to serve. I honestly can't think of anyone better to tell this story than Matt.

God's choices and timing are, as always, flawless.

If you're involved with ministry, I hope you'll set aside time right now to read this book. It will make a compelling case for you to rethink your approach to missions activity and consider the eternal value of making some unexpected connections. The messages are relevant and timely. Best of all, they are essential in working toward our common goal for the Kingdom of God.

Dr. Pete Deison is a pastor, teacher, and president of Park Cities Presbyterian Church Foundation. He has served as a pastor in the Presbyterian Church of America since 1978 and was on the Cru National Team directing the ministry of Campus Crusade for Christ. He now serves as associate pastor of Park Cities Presbyterian Church in Dallas, Texas. He is a featured speaker at the Kanakuk Institute and the author of two books, "The Priority of Knowing God" and "Visits from Heaven."

INTRODUCTION

---◆---

The wooden steps leading up to the mobile home were rotting. The lot was overgrown with weeds. We saw an old shed to the side, flanked by stacks of random household items. After knocking on the door, we could hear a long series of muffled noises inside while we waited for a response.

The person who eventually answered was named Laura. Someone in the community had contacted our organization to tell us about this woman who was struggling on so many levels. A week earlier, I had called to set up a meeting and determine how our team might be able to help.

Laura was noticeably nervous about our visit, but she invited us in. The sadness in her eyes could not be hidden.

She explained that she had been unemployed for several years after an accident left her disabled. She was single, with no family members living in the area. Her friends were sidetracked with their own dysfunction and drama, offering no help with the many challenges that had accumulated in her life.

Laura was financially, physically and emotionally hanging on by a thread, with no one there to catch her if she fell. We could hear the desperation in her voice.

Over the next few months, our team of volunteers got to know Laura better as we worked around her property. We stabilized the stairway that led into the mobile home. Some of our volunteers repaired broken plumbing, while others cleaned up her yard. The transformation was remarkable. But, just like we saw with so many other cases, the biggest change was with Laura herself.

This sullen, withdrawn woman began to show signs of real engagement in conversations. Even some animation. We quickly discovered that Laura had a great deal to say, but no one to say it to. She was starved for conversation. Somehow, the relationships we formed with her—the human connections—had made an infinitely greater impact on Laura than our home repair work did.

Our ministry had been focused on helping people improve their living conditions, but we slowly uncovered a much more ominous issue: *social isolation*. Over and over again, we were introduced to valuable human beings who had become painfully disconnected from the flow of life. Hopeless and alone. Existing in a vacuum with no relationships to sustain them.

On the surface, their needs might look like hunger, addiction or abuse. But underneath it all, isolation was consistently the root of the problem. The similarities were uncanny, and it definitely took us by surprise.

My name is Matt Peacock, and I'm the Executive Director of Partners in Hope—Lake Travis. I served as a pastor for more than 20 years, and I've always had a great passion for helping people in need. With that said, I have a confession.

I never, ever dreamed of being the founder of a nonprofit ministry. Not once. It never crossed my mind. Apparently God didn't see that as a prerequisite—so here I am!

When I launched Partners in Hope in 2011 with a group from our church, it was part of an evolving concept. I clearly knew God was calling me to lead people in mission work but, honestly, the rest was fuzzy. Years went by before we understood the full impact of our efforts and what the Lord had been revealing to us. It was unexpected *and* amazing.

Through connections with many isolated people like Laura, God allowed us to make some radical and compelling discoveries about the process of serving others. I'll admit, those lessons were also a little painful.

I had spent decades doing church missions and outreach work, and it was becoming clear that our standard operating procedures were missing the mark. *Ouch.* Change is never easy, but continuing to do what we'd always done wasn't getting the Kingdom results we wanted.

As time passed, Partners in Hope experienced a ministry reconstruction that totally changed the way we interact with our neighbors in need, as well as how we collaborate with other organizations in our community. The best part? This surprising metamorphosis produced a unique framework for discipleship that has been transformative for everyone involved.

Leave it to God to do things bigger and broader and deeper than anything we could have ever imagined.

The truth is, I can't take any credit for this. I *can* take responsibility for sharing the story so that others like you—in communities around the nation and potentially around the world—can benefit from everything we've learned. That's why I'm writing this book. I want to tell you about the powerful discoveries we've made through Partners in Hope.

I'm genuinely excited to share this journey in the following pages, and I hope the principles that emerge will give you some innovative ideas to use in your Kingdom activities or inspire other possibilities. Perhaps you'll find value in replicating a portion of our model or just applying some of the insights as you seek to do your part in the Kingdom of God. Either way, I've included a list of resources and some tools at the end of the book that can help you further explore our approach to relationship-based ministry.

Thank you for investing the time to learn about the unexpected connections that changed the way we work, while changing so many lives around us. I'm praying that everyone who reads this will be blessed, encouraged and inspired.

CHAPTER ONE

THE
MINISTRY

The funny thing is...I'm not really big on surprises.
God definitely has a sense of humor.

Let's start at the beginning.

I spent many years serving as part of church staffs, and I often took the lead in training church members to participate in outreach. As a group, we'd work on how to share our testimony in three minutes, how to be proactive about meeting our neighbors, and how to disciple new believers. We practiced on each other. The process was different for every church, but sometimes we even scheduled a group outing in the neighborhood to apply what we'd learned in the classroom.

Occasionally someone would bring back an uplifting story of a life transformed. But, more often than not, these students settled back into their normal routines where Christian life seemed to mostly revolve around Sunday mornings. Then the training class would start again with a new set of church members. Basically the same people with different faces. We kept repeating the process, over and over, despite the obvious disconnect.

I was increasingly frustrated by that. We were really good at talking about God on Sundays at church. But on the other six days, outside the walls of our building, we clearly had room for improvement.

Our primary objective for outreach was to share the love of Christ with others. On some level, it seemed so simple, but we were still falling short. Something wasn't working.

That line of thought produced an uncomfortable conclusion.

> *The traditional approach we'd been using for outreach didn't seem very effective for meeting the goal.*

What if we'd been stalled by our own process? What if we were somehow missing the point? As I searched for an answer, my mind kept flashing back to a familiar scene.

Remembering a Pivotal Experience

Through the years, I led mission teams to serve in poor communities along the Texas/Mexico border. Our volunteers—initially a group of 15 but later as many as 40—worked together to improve the living conditions of the people in that area. We made the trip three or four times each year, and our visits ranged from a long weekend to a full week.

Those extended, repetitive visits over a ten-year period allowed us to build strong connections with the residents of that border town. We got to know them, their families, their dreams and their challenges. We watched each other's children grow up. Through it all, we built a level of trust that was a true game-changer.

The people drew hope from the fact that we were committed to helping them long-term. They knew we'd be back. They counted on it and looked forward to it. They found strength in the knowledge that our support and friendship were unchanging, and those relationships opened the door for them to know the Lord.

Right there, at the intersection of outreach and discipleship, we experienced something miraculous.

The changes in those families were readily apparent, but I quickly realized something else. The residents weren't the only ones who gained value from these trips.

The shared act of service also formed the deepest bonds among our volunteers. There's just something magical about a group of people physically demonstrating their love for God, working together to selflessly serve others. Sharing meals. Sharing a space to sleep. Sharing a goal.

All of the people involved with those mission trips—those who were serving and telling the Good News, as well as those who were hearing it—were forever changed by the experience.

As I wrestled with how to solve our church outreach problems, I kept thinking about those trips and the feelings they produced. Our time together was permeated by love in its most pure and perfect form, all while God was teaching us, knocking off our rough edges, plowing our hearts, and helping us to grow. I've often wished I could bottle up that extraordinary feeling of Jesus-powered connection and pour it all over our daily lives. Then it occurred to me: Maybe we could try.

I knew that our traditional outreach efforts on their own weren't enough, but outreach *paired with acts of service and the goal of relationship* had the potential to make a huge difference. If we wanted to *share* the love of Christ, we needed to *show* people the love of Christ. That required time to form authentic connections with them. Time to build trust and have common experiences. Time to have extended conversations—the kind we had during the long days of our regular mission trips and the kind we have daily with the Lord in prayer.

Ongoing discipleship could be the missing spark to light the fire of outreach for the church.

That prompted another uncomfortable reflection: Perhaps we also needed to re-examine our local mission efforts. The church's engagements with the community were more like quick bursts of serving and giving. Often one-time events. We'd work at the food bank on a Saturday. We'd donate books to the orphanage. Then we'd be off to find another project or cause that could use our help.

No doubt about it, these were valuable, much-needed acts of kindness. But one-time, drive-by moments of generosity simply weren't allowing us to make the greatest impact.

God seemed to be showing me a better way. Instead of *transactions*, we had an opportunity to focus on sustained, meaningful *interactions*. And during those interactions, we'd have the time to say and do things that could change lives. This concept of blurring the lines between outreach, discipleship and missions resonated with me on the deepest of levels.

My next thought was, now what? While I knew beyond a shadow of a doubt that God was calling me to lead people in some kind of interaction-based ministry, that's where the clarity ended. I had no idea what it was supposed to look like. But I was absolutely certain God was calling us to take a different approach.

Adjusting Our Approach

While I was contemplating my next move, the leaders of the congregation where I was serving as an associate pastor began to discuss planting a new church. I ended up researching the process, and I started to wonder if that might be an effective platform to apply my new insights. Before long, the idea gained traction. And, in 2008, my trusting family and I set off on a church-planting adventure along with eight families who chose to join us.

We were excited (and a little nervous) about the opportunity to create a very different kind of church. One that focused on the days of the week other than Sunday. One that focused its efforts outside the walls of a church building. One that was fully dedicated to following a unique approach for helping those in need and sharing love throughout the community.

God led us to create a home base for our new church in the Lake Travis region of Texas. Situated in the suburbs west of Austin, this largely rural area once filled with lake cabins was shifting to become a rapidly growing family community. At first glance, these neighborhoods with their sprawling lakeside homes didn't seem like the obvious place to find people in need. We were certainly curious about what God had planned.

Our group began meeting regularly at a local elementary school, and we prayed for direction on how best to reach out to our new neighbors. If the goal of our ministry was to develop relationships and demonstrate love, we needed to get to know the people first.

We started volunteering as a church at local events. We showed up at neighborhood parks to hand out water bottles. We built gardens at the school where we met on Sundays. We deliberately put ourselves in positions to interact in a casual, comfortable way with the people of Lake Travis.

Through our conversations, we learned something important about the residents in this area. Just like many people in Austin, a majority considered themselves spiritual but avoided church because of negative perceptions or experiences in their past. They frequently had stories about "church people" they described as judgmental, hypocritical, cultish, arrogant or uncaring. Any desire they might have had to build a relationship with God was being trampled by those less-than-loving church experiences. Whether those slights were actual or perceived or somewhere in between, that was their story—and they were sticking to it.

Given that perception, what were the chances these people would suspend that negativity and venture out on their own to visit our little church meeting in an elementary school—or any church, for that matter? I was hopeful, but I knew the answer was "slim." The enormity of this challenge was sinking in.

We couldn't afford to take a passive approach.

> *If it wasn't realistic to think that Lake Travis residents would come to us, we would keep going to them. Wherever they were.*

In spite of the uphill battle, our team maintained a genuine enthusiasm for reaching out and loving people, even the ones who were skeptical of the church.

Getting Connected

As we brainstormed about more direct ways to serve the people in our community, we made a connection with Lake Travis Crisis Ministries, a local nonprofit and food bank. The organizers there agreed to put us in touch with a few families who needed help improving their living conditions. That seemed like a good place to start. At least it would give us a foot in the door, so to speak, to begin building personal connections with people we hoped to show the love of Jesus. We soon discovered that Lake Travis did have some pockets of older, occasionally run-down homes in sharp contrast to the million-dollar estates, and we were eager to provide our assistance.

We followed up with the families referred to us and offered to do whatever they needed around their homes. Yard work. Minor home repairs. Hauling away trash.

No matter what task we took on, we spent time getting to know the people. We kept our focus. The relationships were more important than the renovations.

We wanted them to feel God's love through our presence, and we always gave them an open invitation to worship with us on Sundays.

In the spring of 2010, we were ready to gain some serious momentum. We had been getting a steady stream of referrals from the food bank, and additional opportunities started coming our way from other sources. The adults at our church were willing to use some of their vacation time from work to participate in our efforts. As summer arrived, we had extra volunteers among our families with children out of school and college kids at home for a few months. That's when we invented SNOW Days (Serving Neighbors on Wednesdays).

Every Wednesday that summer, our church family showed up to help someone in the community and demonstrate God's love. Those days of working together and sharing our skills with people in need were immensely rewarding for all of us.

Making a Difference

One particular story from that summer really stands out for me, even today.

I received a call from the principal of the elementary school where our church met on Sundays. She wanted to see if we might be able to offer some assistance to one of the families from her school. A single mother of two named Kim had just gone through a divorce, and she was also battling cancer. The principal explained that this typically confident woman had not asked for help, but people at school picked up some clues that she might be struggling to keep up with the basic demands of life. I assured her that we would reach out to Kim and see if we could be of service.

Once I hung up, I couldn't help but wonder why the principal had not contacted someone for help at the large church that was literally across the street from the school. This church had a large campus, more than a thousand members, and a big presence in the community. Our church?

We had fewer than 50 members and stored all of our supplies in a trailer that we parked at a friend's business during the week. Each Sunday, our "pop-up church" emerged when we unloaded the contents of our trailer into a school cafeteria.

And yet, for some reason, the principal contacted us.

I called Kim that same day to introduce myself and tell her about our team. Although she initially declined my offer of help ("Oh no, we're fine. Thank you!"), our conversation continued. Before we finished, Kim timidly mentioned a few things around her house that had been neglected during her time of personal and physical crisis. I could still hear a touch of hesitation in her voice, but we set up a time to get together.

On the scheduled day, our team caravanned into a friendly neighborhood located a few blocks from the elementary school. The well-kept houses all looked basically the same, and we were searching for the one that displayed obvious, external signs of "need." An overgrown yard. A collapsed porch.

When we pulled up in front of a nice home that was indistinguishable from its neighbors, I could tell the team members were confused. Did we have the wrong address? Could the people inside this house really need help with improving their living conditions? We were about to find out.

Kim greeted us warmly at the door and admitted she was still in disbelief that we were there. Noticeably weak from the cancer treatments, she made her way back to the sofa before telling us about the things around the house that could possibly use our attention. She smiled as she watched our volunteers launch into activity around her.

Life had thrown Kim some serious curveballs, and she was utterly overwhelmed. Her unwelcome shift into survival mode meant that normal home maintenance had not been a priority, but every day she felt anxious about falling further behind. We hoped to change that.

Our team spent the day cleaning out Kim's garage, washing the car, mowing and trimming the lawn, fixing a leaky faucet, replacing a broken window blind, storing things in the attic, and taking other items to Goodwill. Throughout that time, our volunteers also took turns sitting with Kim and talking with her about her children, her work, and her health challenges.

Kim repeatedly thanked us for being there that day and told us she felt like a weight was being lifted off her shoulders. She also shared what she considered the most amazing part of the experience.

The strangers who showed up on her front porch
at 9:00 that morning were now her friends.

She still couldn't believe that our team had such a sincere interest in her life and invested the time to help her.

As we were finishing the last of the projects and gathering up our tools, a woman rushed through the front door. She anxiously scanned the room, looking for Kim among our team of volunteers.

"Who are these people?" she asked with a nervous smile. "What are they doing here?"

Kim laughed and introduced us to her mother, Bonnie. Since Bonnie looked completely bewildered by our presence, I took a moment to sit down and chat with her. I told her about the work we had done that day at the house and explained how our church was passionate about the mission to serve neighbors in Lake Travis. As I spoke, I could see Bonnie holding back the tears. She expressed deep gratitude for our willingness to help her daughter.

Then Bonnie told me something I never expected. She mentioned that she was a member of another large church in the area. In fact, she served on the missions committee and was just on her way home from a meeting with that group. I could tell from her expression that she recognized the awkward irony of the situation. Still, she graciously thanked us again for sharing God's love with her family in a beautiful, tangible way.

Reflecting on the Day

My mind was flooded with questions that night.

> *How could someone like Kim fall through the cracks,*
> *particularly when her mother is an active church member?*

Was she overlooked because she lived in a nice house in a prominent area? Did pride prevent her from asking for the help she desperately needed? Did she feel ashamed or embarrassed that she couldn't "keep it together" during a stressful time? Why was Kim's mother so surprised by our actions when she served on a missions committee? And again, why did the school principal reach out to us for help instead of contacting someone at a much larger church?

If not for some observant people at school and a proactive principal, Kim would still be suffering through this difficult season of life all by herself. Alone. Inside her lovely home. Pretending everything was fine. Feeling completely isolated from the world.

God showed us something important that day that we wouldn't completely comprehend until much later.

Taking the Next Steps

In the Fall of 2010, the adults in our church family were back at work and the kids returned to school. Serving every Wednesday was no longer an option, but we made the commitment to volunteer as a group one Saturday every month.

The problem? Referrals were pouring in after the SNOW Days noticeably increased our visibility in the Lake Travis neighborhoods. The scope of the need was much larger than we imagined, and the workload quickly exceeded the capacity of our small congregation.

It was obvious that we couldn't handle all of this on our own. We began recruiting people from the area to participate in our serving efforts throughout 2011. We discovered that volunteers from the community would happily show up to help on a certain day if we made the process easy—organizing the projects, providing all the materials, and giving clear instructions about the work to be done. But even with outside volunteers, we were falling short. We simply needed the connections to additional resources.

> *I started to realize that this enormous effort might be a community ministry rather than a single church ministry.*

If we wanted to touch more hearts, we would have to do it as a nonprofit organization. Partners in Hope—Lake Travis was established that fall.

The next two years were extremely busy. I was a full-time pastor/church planter, while also working part-time to establish and run the nonprofit. Despite the hectic pace, we were grateful for the opportunity to serve dozens of people and facilitate hundreds of volunteers in the Lake Travis area.

In 2013, after six years of leading our planted church, I felt God was urging me to pass the leadership baton on to someone else. I processed this with the church elders and, in October, announced my resignation to be effective at year-end. Truthfully, I didn't have a plan about where to go next, but I assumed the Lord would guide me to another congregation where I could serve in a pastoral position.

That's when it happened.

I was immersed in searching for another church leadership role when God stepped in to redirect my path. It felt like the emotional equivalent of someone grabbing me by the shoulders and shaking me. The cage-rattling came with a crystal-clear message: "Hey, Matt! Don't you see what's happening here? Your involvement with the nonprofit wasn't a temporary assignment."

Wait, what? Needless to say, this caught me off guard. I'm a pastor. I can say without hesitation that I never saw myself running a nonprofit full-time. My ministry was with the church.

God disagreed. Loud and clear. So who was I to argue? Of course, I *did* actually argue. I put it off for a month, just to "make sure." And that went well… Nope. Not well at all. I finally moved from refusal, to reluctance, to mystified embracing!

Leading the Nonprofit

At the beginning of 2014, I made the commitment to become the Director of Partners in Hope. Being able to devote my full attention to the cause gave it a real jump-start, and I was excited to take on each new level of growth. As things quickly accelerated, I also began to get more vision and clarity from the Lord about our purpose. Things I had thought about and wanted to do were now actually happening.

My weeks were jam-packed with a diverse set of tasks: communicating with the Board of Directors to get funding for our work, representing the organization throughout the community, meeting with families in need, coordinating volunteers and managing projects. No matter how much I tried to multi-task, I was still the bottleneck for getting things done. I knew I couldn't continue managing all aspects of the organization by myself, so it was time to get some help.

In 2015, we doubled the size of our organization. In other words, we hired a second staff member as an Assistant Director & Volunteer Coordinator. The additional bandwidth allowed Partners in Hope to serve more people and, frankly, it gave us the courage to say "yes" to opportunities I couldn't have tackled on my own. Using our divide-and-conquer approach, we steadily expanded our connections in the Lake Travis area.

During that time period, I remember being so amazed by the constantly evolving ministry that became Partners in Hope. Our journey was shaped by the two important discoveries I've described so far.

First, the time we spent with people like Laura showed me that God wanted us to focus on people instead of projects.

That's why relationships became the centerpiece of our mission.

Second, through our experiences with those like Kim, God opened our eyes to see that people are out there suffering all alone. Their problems and issues aren't always visible, or they are hidden behind other things, which means they're easily overlooked by neighbors, colleagues and community members. People can end up battling difficult situations all by themselves. This was a huge reminder for us, as a nonprofit, to look beneath the surface in identifying those in need. Loneliness can easily be camouflaged.

By devotedly following these new insights, Partners in Hope seemed to be right on track. Little did we know that God was about to shake things up in a huge way.

CHAPTER TWO

THE CRISIS

As someone who needs time by myself periodically, I still recognize how unbearable it must be to always be alone. I'm grateful God has given me so many people to crowd my space.

In early 2016, we started to hear more discussion in the media about the physical and mental impact of extreme loneliness. There were countless news articles, research studies, and documentaries on this topic. Each one vividly described the devastating effects of being separated from others—a phenomenon we had seen firsthand.

When life becomes overwhelming, some people tend to withdraw and pull away. They can't (or won't) ask for help. And things get worse from there, in a tragic downward spiral of separation. Those were the people we had been repeatedly led to help over the years.

> *We knew exactly what that intense loneliness looked like.*
> *We'd seen the impact. We just didn't know it was a full-blown*
> *epidemic with an official name: social isolation.*

The Revelation

With the luxury of 20/20 hindsight, we reflected on the stories from some of our ministry clients.

The man who lost his wife of 38 years to cancer continued to smoke incessantly...*because he was isolated.* The young woman who escaped domestic violence and was paralyzed by fear every time she left her home was suffering...*from isolation.* The disabled military veteran who had fallen into a deep depression because of his injuries was struggling... *with isolation.* The elderly woman—suddenly alone with the passing of her soul-mate husband—was facing physical deterioration and mounting bills...*in isolation.*

Right then and there, God was leading us to connect the dots.

Maybe we had been trying to solve the wrong problem. What if our purpose at Partners in Hope wasn't really about building relationships with people by improving their living conditions? What if God was challenging us to help end social isolation?

You can probably imagine my reaction to that thought. Social isolation was considered by the experts to be an enormous, all-encompassing social crisis, and we were a little nonprofit. Surely God didn't expect us to take on something of this magnitude with its epic implications. Or did He?

That season was simultaneously humbling *and* terrifying for me.

If the Lord really was pushing us to help solve this kind of mammoth problem, we needed to learn more about social isolation. I want to share a snapshot of our findings in the pages that follow.

The Research

One of the pioneers of research in this area was Dr. John T. Cacioppo with the University of Chicago. He and a colleague actually founded the entire field of Social Neuroscience in 1992, and his work paved the way for the scientific studies we currently have about social isolation.

Cacioppo made an important distinction from the outset:

- **Social isolation** is the *objective* physical separation from other people.
- **Loneliness** is the *subjective* pain and distress of feeling separate from others.

I thought it was interesting that these concepts were similar but not identical. In retrospect, that made sense. We all know someone who feels lonely while surrounded by people. Others purposely isolate themselves and don't feel lonely at all. With Partners in Hope, we were being called to help those at the intersection of the two concepts: people experiencing the psychological feelings of loneliness because of a physical separation from others.

The Impact

One of the best articles about the effects of social isolation appeared in *The New York Times* (December 22, 2016) and was written by a doctor named Dhruv Khullar. Dr. Khullar is a resident physician at Massachusetts General Hospital and Harvard Medical School. In the article, he explained in great detail that social isolation is "increasingly recognized as having dire physical, mental and emotional consequences." He cited extensive studies to support that claim, linking social isolation to a wide range of ailments:

- Higher blood pressure
- Increased stress hormones
- Disrupted sleep patterns
- Elevated levels of inflammation
- Increased risk of depression, anxiety, and schizophrenia
- Altered immune systems
- Decreased resistance to infection
- Accelerated cognitive and functional decline
- Significantly elevated risk of heart disease, stroke, metastatic cancer, and Alzheimer's disease

To put all of that in perspective, consider these additional findings:

- Social isolation increases health risks as much as smoking 15 cigarettes per day or abusing alcohol. *(Brigham Young University, 2015)*

- Social isolation is twice as harmful to physical and mental health as obesity. *(Brigham Young University, 2015)*
- Socially isolated people have a 26% higher risk of dying—32% higher if they live alone. *(Journal of the Association for Psychological Science, 2015)*

I still find these facts to be absolutely staggering.

> *While lonely people need the support and comfort of relationships, socially isolated people need an immediate, full-blown intervention to protect their health.*

If that sounds a bit on the melodramatic side, let me assure you it is not.

The Proof

I vividly remember our time working with a woman named Shelley. She was in her late 60s (although she looked much older) and couldn't have weighed more than 80 pounds. She lived in a long-neglected trailer home with 18 cats (yes, 18!) and her 40-year-old son who suffered from a long list of issues. It was a sad scenario of dysfunction and hopelessness.

The homeowners' association was threatening to fine or evict Shelley if she didn't upgrade the skirting around her trailer home to be masonry. The price tag? Around $2,000. That wasn't even an option for Shelley. Although she had a full-time job as a cashier for a local store, she was living paycheck to paycheck. Lake Travis Crisis Ministries recognized her struggle and referred her to Partners in Hope.

From our first meeting with Shelley, we knew God was giving us an enormous challenge. We learned that her life had been treacherous, filled with abuse and co-dependence. In the time we knew her, Shelley's adult able-bodied son rarely had steady work and mostly stayed in his room. She had spent years fighting to keep her head above water, but the battle with the homeowners' association was pulling her under.

Outwardly, Shelley appeared frightened and untrusting, but we could tell bitterness and anger were lurking below the surface. She felt like life had given her a raw deal. Worst of all, she had no support network. No friends. No other family members. She was trying to navigate this crisis all on her own, the same way she'd always done it. If she hadn't been desperate, I don't think she would have been willing to accept our help.

Shelley was far too embarrassed about her living conditions to let us inside her trailer. Even outside, we were overwhelmed by the horrifying smell, and I knew we couldn't send a team in there without special breathing equipment.

Given that situation, we focused on upgrading the exterior of the trailer and cleaning up the lot, while continually encouraging her toward healthier options for her environment. Amazingly, one of our volunteers even spent several weeks (and her own money) to take all of Shelley's cats in to the vet for sterilization.

The more time we spent working in Shelley's yard, the more insight we gained about her situation.

A disproportionate amount of her paycheck was being used by her son, so she wasn't eating well. Her health seemed to be declining. Plus, her work hours were surprisingly lonely.

The managers at the store where she worked had strict policies that limited employee interactions with patrons and each other. Shelley couldn't afford to lose her job, so she avoided anything but short, super-ficial conversations with the people in the store. She kept her distance and hid behind a thick, emotional barrier. And, at the end of the day, she went home to an empty room with deplorable conditions.

It seemed like Shelley had already been
suffocated by isolation.

We regularly invited her to join us at our monthly dinners and community events, but she never said yes. Not once in three years. We did everything in our power to connect her with the outside world, but she seemed too hurt and scarred from her past to even consider devel-oping relationships. From the comments she made, I'm pretty sure she never felt worthy of friends.

One morning, I got a call from the county hospice program, letting me know that Shelley had been referred to them and wouldn't survive much longer. Breast cancer had viciously invaded her body. She didn't have the time or money to seek treatment, so she had been ignoring the signs for months. Now it was too late.

When I went to visit Shelley at the trailer, she was reclined in a portable hospital bed parked in the middle of her living room. Her son was nowhere to be found. I sat with her about an hour and tried to give her some words of comfort without much of a response. I hope she knew I was there.

Soon after that, Shelley died. Alone. Basically the same way she had lived her life.

Social isolation stole her physical, mental and emotional health. It killed her. We already knew that this was a tragic, deadly disease before we started reading about all the research that proved it.

The Causes

God was clearly revealing to us the scope and urgency of this problem. If we wanted to respond effectively, we needed to gain clarity about the factors contributing to the crisis. What we learned about were three societal shifts in the way people relate to each other. When those three shifts collided, they created the perfect storm for an isolation epidemic. And it was obvious that God had been warning us to stay away from that storm all along.

1. Fractured Families

God designed families to be our greatest source of joy, as well as our primary support system during daily challenges and times of tragedy. From a broader perspective, the Lord cherished the concept of family so much that He used it as a foundation to frame our relationship with Him. Ephesians 1:5 tells us: *"God decided in advance to adopt us into His own family by bringing us to Himself through Jesus Christ. This is what He wanted to do, and it gave Him great pleasure."*

Here and in heaven, families are a primary building block for our lives and our faith. Unfortunately, the building blocks of our earthly families look vastly different today than they did just a few generations ago.

Divorce rates are high, and single-parent households are prevalent. Birth rates are steadily declining, as more people choose not to have children or even get married. As for those who still belong to a relatively traditional family unit, the concept of quality time together is vanishing. People are putting in more hours at the office, taking on multiple jobs, or pursuing opportunities that take them far from home.

Bottom line, families are now scattered, stretched and sometimes unrecognizable. Further pushing us in that direction are the sizable shifts in our culture that seem to reinforce those dynamics.

Simply put, our existence as families is splintering.

With so many outside pressures, people are less likely to have a parent, child or sibling present for support in their daily lives—helping to keep smaller issues from piling up or stepping in to provide assistance when things go terribly wrong. And without the life raft of family connections, many people are sinking into crisis.

2. *Fractured Relationships*

When families function in this more fractured manner, children end up with a lack of role models to demonstrate healthy relationships. They grow up thinking that disconnectedness is the norm. Separation is the standard.

While the lack of positive relationship role models is devastating enough, there's another thorny consequence. That gap is often filled by negative examples that actually promote isolation. When people eventually share why they chose to pull away from the rest of the world, the culprits are typically dysfunctional relationships and difficulty believing that others can be trusted.

That's not at all what God intended. Throughout the Bible, we can find plenty of instructions about how we should care for one another.

In 1 Thessalonians 5:14, Paul shares some essential guidelines for being in relationships with others: *"We urge you, brothers and sisters, warn those who are idle and disruptive, encourage the disheartened, help the weak, be patient with everyone."*

This verse highlights the importance of having people in our lives who can support us as we go through different seasons. Sometimes we need accountability and someone who can speak truth into us. Sometimes we need encouragement to overcome disappointment or sadness. And other times, we need someone who can literally care for us because we're flat on our backs and totally dependent.

This verse also points out the standards we should apply when helping others. We should invest the time necessary to understand their needs and be willing to support them in meeting those. We should adopt a posture of patience rather than demanding that others be on our time-table. And in a healthy, caring relationship, we genuinely want the best for the other person.

Suffice it to say, God set the bar pretty high when it comes to expectations for relationships and, as a society, we're falling short of that. Part of the problem, as I see it, is that face-to-face communication is becoming a lost art. Technology gets at least some of the blame for that disjointedness.

While we now have the digital capacity to connect with people across the planet, our ability to emotionally connect with someone standing right in front of us has eroded.

That's deadly when it comes to building and maintaining relationships.

In-person conversations do require a completely different skill set than the digital shortcuts. While we listen to the words being said in person, we are also expected to "read" facial expressions, body language, tone of voice, and all the other nonverbal cues in real-time. Then we're supposed to respond...immediately. We can't process the information, type, delete, reword, and send a reply 30 minutes later. It's harder—and it's harder to get it right.

Somehow, our extraordinary digital connections have generated the greatest sense of personal disconnectedness our world has ever experienced. Relationships are becoming more dysfunctional, and people are feeling isolated and alone.

3. Fractured Communities

Years ago, the borders of our neighborhoods naturally created a close community. All the kids on the block went to the same school, and everyone shopped at the corner grocery store. Life wasn't perfect, but the societal structure created patterns of repeated interactions with the same group of people. The outcome was strong, lasting community bonds.

The Bible reminds us about the compounded value of connecting with the people who live in our immediate vicinity. In Acts 2:42-47, Luke described that power:

"They devoted themselves to the apostles' teaching and to fellowship, to the breaking of bread and to prayer. Everyone was filled with awe at the many wonders and signs performed by the apostles. All the believers were together and had everything in common. They sold property and possessions to give to anyone who had need. Every day they continued to meet together in the temple courts. They broke bread in their homes and ate together with glad and sincere hearts, praising God and enjoying the favor of all the people. And the Lord added to their number daily those who were being saved."

Ideally, our community is a place where we "do life together" connected by the Spirit of God. Sharpening each other. Caring for each other. Sharing, teaching and encouraging our neighbors in a way that points them to God and magnifies the beauty of His truth. When everyone in the community seeks and serves the Lord together, it can be a transformative process.

Today, living in the same zip code no longer translates into the loving sense of community God had in mind. Neighbors are more mobile. They might travel farther for work or school and, many times, they settle for "manufactured communities" defined by common interests rather than geography.

Those can provide people with a sense of belonging, but it's more of a fleeting sensation. The relationships that form in neighborhoods through constant proximity to the same people, day in and day out, are vastly different. And now, those community relationships are becoming extinct.

When we closely examine these three factors—the fracturing of our families, personal relationships, and communities—it's clear to see how social isolation crept in and was able to permeate so many lives.

The Church Perspective

In the midst of our exploration to better understand how social isolation was impacting the people we served, we recognized the problem had another angle. This perfect storm of societal changes was transforming the landscape for our churches, too. It was all part of the same equation.

Think for a moment about social isolation as it relates to churches.

Smaller neighborhood churches with one or two hundred members were once a staple of community life. Everyone knew everyone else, and it felt like family. If you weren't in the pews on Sunday morning, you could feel confident that others would call to check on you and, more than likely, show up with a casserole. The relationships and the connections were rock-solid.

Today, many of these small houses of worship are declining or being replaced with larger churches—even some mega-churches that can have thousands of members and multiple gathering times. People will commute from all over town to attend their services, often to hear a charismatic pastor or to learn about a topic of interest.

Even if members show up every week, they may never see the same people twice. That makes it tougher and tougher to be part of a life-giving community.

> *Now churches have to be very intentional to counteract the disconnection and avoid losing people in the shuffle.*

The light switch flipped on for me as I thought about that sad progression. I had been so perplexed by the fact that someone like Kim could be overlooked but, in this context, I could see how it happened.

If we don't recognize the people we see on Sunday mornings, it's much less obvious when someone is missing. The classic formula for neighbors checking in and caring for each other no longer applies, which means people living steps away from the packed worship service could be suffering all alone. No one has a clear way to identify the problem of isolation in a world with fractured communities.

The Evidence

To illustrate the depth of this problem, I want to tell you about a woman named Audrey. She and her husband were retired and living on a fixed income. They had been in the same house for more than 40 years. On a windy day in November, the large storage shed behind their house caught fire and burned to the ground. The back portion of their property suddenly became a jumbled mess of charred household items, trash, and partially burned shrubbery.

Audrey and her husband were not physically able to clean up the yard, but they also didn't have the funds to hire assistance. Shortly after that, they were referred to Partners in Hope.

I reached out to Audrey, and we had several good conversations about the possibility that one of our teams could help with the property clean-up. When I checked back with her to schedule a time for our visit, Audrey explained she couldn't do anything at that time. Her husband was having a health crisis and had been admitted to the Intensive Care Unit of the local hospital.

I had only met this couple a few times, and the husband was never able to converse with me during my visits. Now I was in the awkward position of trying to support a family in crisis that I barely knew. Audrey faithfully spent six weeks by her husband's side at the hospital, until the day after Christmas when he passed away.

Several days later, I attended the funeral. Audrey's husband was a 94-year-old World War II veteran and received full military honors with a 21-gun salute. Everyone there was moved when the uniformed officers folded the flag that had been draped over the casket and presented it to his grieving wife.

I had only been home from the funeral for a few hours when my phone rang. It was Audrey, and she was hysterical. After laying her beloved husband to rest, she arrived back at her house to find a large, bold sign erected in her front lawn. The homeowners' association was giving her formal notice that she had 28 days to clean up her yard, or she would be faced with a heavy fine and potential legal action.

> *Audrey was having a crisis on what was already one*
> *of the worst days of her life, and she called me.*
> *I had only known her for six weeks.*

It seemed there was no one else. No family. No friends. No neighbors she could call. Audrey was desperate for help and feeling very alone.

For me, this really showed the deep roots of isolation in our society. The neighborhood organization had no idea that their violation sign would be the first thing seen by a widow coming home from her husband's funeral. They didn't know her or what was going on in her life. And they didn't feel any *obligation* to know. The concept of being "neighborly" got lost in translation.

Time and time again, we encountered people like Audrey who were suffering from the invisible, insidious evil of isolation. And every time, it was jolting. This epidemic was frighteningly complex. How in the world was Partners in Hope supposed to address a challenge of this scale? How do we even get started?

I certainly didn't have the answer, but I knew God did.

CHAPTER THREE

THE SOLUTION

*I never thought I'd write about the Bible and "Where's Waldo?"
in the same paragraph, but it happened.*

One thing we know for sure is that God created us for connection. From the very beginning, with Adam and Eve. When He created man, He declared that "it was not good for man to be alone." God wanted Adam and Eve to experience life together, and He wanted to spend time with them as well. The book of Genesis tells us that God walked with them in the garden and treasured the relationship.

Then came Genesis 3. When Adam and Eve broke God's commandment, they damaged the relationship. They hid and *isolated themselves*. From that day forward, all of mankind has struggled to relate to one another and to God.

> *This brokenness was the precursor for the epidemic of isolation that we see in the world today.*

For us as Christians, we already know the overarching solution. Isolated people desperately need a relationship with God that makes them part of His community, the Kingdom. That connection allows them to trade in their loneliness and isolation for an existence where the Holy Spirit is always with them, and they are surrounded by brothers and sisters in Christ who care about what happens to them.

It's like an orphan being adopted into a big, loving family. Everything changes.

So what does that mean for us at Partners in Hope? Our ultimate, long-term goal is to bring more people into the Kingdom of God. It has to be the ministry's bottom line, the driving force. With that said, the practical strategies to achieve this goal through our nonprofit had been continuously changing.

I've shared with you how our organization's short-term mission shifted over time. To serve our neighbors. To love them. To build ongoing relationships with them. In light of what we'd learned about social isolation, I knew we'd continue to transform.

I could feel the sense of urgency surrounding this crisis. As I thought about our broader Kingdom goal, scriptures I had known for decades began to speak to me in a different way. More personally. I was drawn to the New Testament, and **two unmistakable messages** kept jumping out at me.

1. *We're called to pursue isolated people for the Kingdom of God.*

Have you ever feverishly scanned one of those "Where's Waldo?" images, searching in vain for his signature red-and-white hat and glasses? About the time you're convinced Waldo must be missing, you spot him. It seems so obvious. And you wonder, how did I *not* see that before?

That's basically how I felt as I stared at my Bible. Over and over, Jesus gave us examples for how to bring people into the Kingdom of God. He frequently sought out those who were rejected or devalued, without any concern for optics or political correctness. Looking at that through the lens of our latest research findings, I recognized something new.

> *Jesus was actively reaching out to people who suffered from social isolation—the despised, the shunned, the outcasts.*

He also took His disciples straight to the people they would typically avoid, which often raised some eyebrows. Despite their appalled reactions, Jesus wasn't the least bit concerned about chatting at the well with a Samaritan woman who was obviously the town pariah. He chose to have dinner at Zacchaeus' house, even though the tax collector had no friends and a terrible reputation, considering his questionable business practices.

Jesus' parables echoed the same theme. In Luke, He illustrates the concept of the Kingdom of God with a story about a man who prepares a great feast. When the invited guests make excuses for not attending, he sends his servants out to specifically find the people who are isolated—crippled, lame, and blind—and bring them back to sit at the table. In Matthew, He describes the shepherd who leaves his flock of 99 sheep to find the one that's separated and lost. He asks his friends to help him celebrate when the isolated sheep returns home.

There it was, plain as day. On so many levels, Jesus was laser-focused on *saving isolated people.* I had heard those Bible stories my whole life, but I never looked at them quite this way before. It was obvious. Just like Waldo and his hat. Once you know it's there, you can't NOT see it.

I wanted to translate that insight into our work with Partners in Hope, while acknowledging the differences between then and now. Isolated people today aren't necessarily as much outcasts as they are simply hidden in a culture that allows them to fade into the background and not be noticed. We didn't know if other local organizations were also pursuing these "invisible neighbors," but God was calling us to serve them. We knew He was helping us to clarify our mission.

The other thing that resonated with me as I looked at the Bible stories with fresh eyes was the active approach Jesus took to bring people into the Kingdom. He didn't passively invite them; He actively *pursued* them. He reached out to them, wherever they were, in their separate, disconnected, isolated circumstances. He searched for them and initiated the relationships.

Looking back at those examples, I found it interesting that Jesus was actually showing us two important things.

He was helping us define who we should be pursuing for the Kingdom of God. But He was also demonstrating precisely how to become people who are passionate about pursuing others.

Jesus understood that isolated people had no context for why they should want to become part of the Kingdom of God, much less how to join. The responsibility for making those connections and pursuing others lies with those of us who are already part of the Kingdom. That reminder felt like an affirmation of the shifts we made at Partners in Hope, going from transactional serving to relationship building. It also felt like a challenge to step up our game.

God was calling us to help build His Kingdom, bringing a new level of passion and perseverance to our pursuit of isolated people in Lake Travis.

2. We can do the most good for the Kingdom of God if all the parts of the Kingdom work together.

In Romans 12:4-5, Paul provides us with a familiar metaphor.

"Just as there are many parts to our bodies, so it is with Christ's body. We are all parts of it, and it takes every one of us to make it complete, for we each have different work to do. So we belong to each other, and each needs all the others."

Churches commonly apply that metaphor about the body of Christ within their congregations as they discuss spiritual gifts and the unique differences among their members. Individuals with their own skills and talents synergistically come together as a united group to become the hands and feet of Christ in the world. But should the application be limited to local churches?

With my new vantage point in the nonprofit arena, I started to think about that serving metaphor in a different light. The best way for me to explain that is by describing the traditional paradigm for serving neighbors in need that exists in most communities throughout the country.

The Serving Paradigm

The process starts with those who need help. Sadly, most isolated people don't ask for assistance until things get really bad. They painfully exist alone, under the radar, until the crisis occurs. The roof caves in. The food runs out. The plumbing is broken. When they have no other choice, they reach out for help.

At that moment—the tipping point—a crack in the isolation allows a tiny ray of light to shine on their invisible suffering.

Who do these isolated people contact first? Since they require assistance with a specific need, they're likely to bypass the local church and turn to nonprofit organizations with the expertise and resources to solve their immediate problem.

For example:

- Hunger
- Homelessness
- Addiction
- Unemployment
- Medical Emergency
- Mental Health Distress
- Crisis Pregnancy
- Natural Disaster Recovery

These nonprofits with their areas of specialization become the **primary doorway** *for the once-hidden needs of many isolated people to become visible within the community.*

They are on the front lines to get those initial calls or referrals from agencies.

Armed with requests for help, the nonprofits then reach out to local churches to get financial support and volunteers to fuel their operations. Churches collect an offering, donate money, and send people to assist. The nonprofits operate as the gatekeepers and make the rules for funneling support back to those who need it.

Traditional Serving Paradigm
How Communities Support People in Need

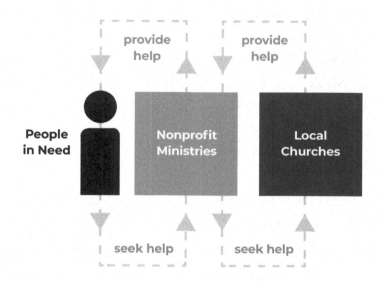

One interesting thing about this process is the distinct *separation* between churches and the people in need. In some respects, the nonprofit doorway is also a *barrier*. The nonprofits handle the heavy lifting, and the church members play more of a supporting role. That makes it hard for church members to fully understand the people who are being helped or the true scope of need in their community. They often feel detached from the process and the impact of their giving.

This traditional paradigm can also fail people in need from a long-term perspective. They might get a hot meal, a safe place to sleep or a new resource, but a limited fix doesn't solve the bigger issue and the lingering problem of isolation that we'd become all too familiar with. It's treating the symptoms without curing the disease. The process had a serious *disconnect*.

The Silo Effect

That's such an interesting coincidence. The words we had been using to describe our neighbors in need—isolated, separated, disconnected—were also words that seemed to apply to the process of serving within our communities.

We could envision lonely people existing in their own silos, set apart from others. What we didn't realize is that nonprofits and churches fall victim to the silo effect as well.

We already know that nonprofits in a community are typically organized by type of service offered. People dealing with addiction can't get the help they need at the food bank. People who want to learn English as a second language don't seek assistance at the homeless shelter. If they did, they'd be referred to another organization. In other words, getting assistance is usually *not* a one-stop-shopping experience. All of these services are typically provided by separate organizations, through different silos.

The Silo Effect

Nonprofit Ministries

Abuse | Addiction | Illiteracy | Natural Disaster | Poverty | Hunger | Homelessness

Churches are susceptible to the same tendency. Sometimes they have a sense of friendly competition with other churches in the neighborhood, but they rarely team up to work together. Or if they do, it's often for a transactional, short-term project. Each church may want to feel a sense of ownership about championing a particular cause. "The other church supports the agency that helps domestic abuse victims. Let's pick something else."

Silos at work, yet again.

The Silo Effect

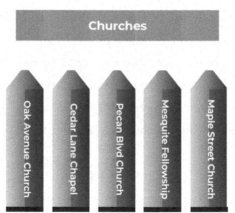

All of these groups wanted to support isolated neighbors in need, but they were trying to reach that goal while operating in their own silos. Separation and isolation had invaded the whole process. It was everywhere.

Which brings me back to the main point.

Jesus told us that we can do the most good for the Kingdom of God when all the parts of the body of Christ work together. So far, we had been limited in our impact for the Kingdom by our limited interpretation of that metaphor. I'll explain.

Many a sermon has been taught on the passages in Romans 12 and 1 Corinthians about the body of Christ, and church members are comfortable thinking about that kind of unity within the scope of their own congregations. But rarely are those passages applied to the Kingdom—to all Kingdom ministries including churches *and* nonprofit ministries—working together in an integrated way. People simply hadn't made the leap to consider their churches as *a part of* the body of Christ rather than *all of it*. Myopic thinking was holding us back.

Connection was still the answer to the isolation problem, but the real challenge would be applying that answer to the people serving just as much as those being served.

God was calling us to help smash those invisible boundaries and think about working collectively as the Kingdom in an exponentially bigger way: a silo-less, coordinated effort across all mission-focused organizations. Somehow we needed to restructure the way volunteers in our community work together to pursue our isolated neighbors.

The Challenge

The two messages from the New Testament that I highlighted in this chapter formed the basis of our new action plan at Partners in Hope.

First, we wanted to adopt a more effective model for our own organization to pursue and connect with our isolated neighbors.

And second, we wanted to change the community serving paradigm to one that serves the Kingdom, helping to dissolve the silos and create a more seamless, community-wide approach to connect with those in need.

Our consistent message would be reminding nonprofit ministries and local churches about our common goal: to connect more people with the body of Christ.

Through teamwork, we had the potential to accelerate the process of connecting more people to God's Kingdom.

We were excited about the possibilities, but we knew restructuring the paradigm for Kingdom service was going to be difficult. What we didn't know? *Understanding* a shared mission doesn't always translate to *being willing and ready* to take on the challenge. We had our work cut out for us.

The next two chapters describe how we moved forward in each of those areas.

CHAPTER FOUR

THE MODEL

We worked hard to let the community know about our ministry for making physical improvements to people's homes. Now the challenge is explaining that's not at all what we're about.

We're called to pursue isolated people for the Kingdom of God.

In light of everything we learned about social isolation, we felt like God was calling us to further shift the focus of Partners in Hope and adjust the model we use to serve our clients.

One thing we knew for sure, the idea of connection was at the heart of our new purpose. Everything revolved around it.

We used that concept as the foundation to reframe our work:

- **Connect** with socially isolated people in Lake Travis to build ongoing relationships.
- **Connect** isolated people with a network of local organizations that provide the resources and support they need to become an integrated part of the community.
- **Connect** volunteers from local churches and faith-based nonprofits to work together as interactive partners in serving isolated people *(more on that in Chapter Five)*.
- **Connect** isolated people with opportunities for sustained relationships through a church family and, ultimately, as members of God's Kingdom.
- **Connect** isolated people with opportunities to genuinely become engaged in the community.

We'd already taken an unusual path by emphasizing relationships with our mission activities. Now we were jumping head-first into a whole new category: connection makers and isolation fighters.

Instead of being defined as a group that helps to improve the living conditions of neighbors in need, we knew God was calling us to a different mission with an emerging model. Living conditions were just the means, not the end. As of 2017, Partners in Hope became an organization that *connects isolated people in Lake Travis who desire physical, emotional and spiritual help with people who will help.*

What was the first step?

As I reflected on the connections that would be the driving force of our updated nonprofit, I thought specifically about the nuances involved with this concept. It's possible to connect with someone briefly and keep going, but we wanted to cultivate something meaningful and more pervasive.

We had basically been hoping for organic connections with our clients in the past. Even if we built good relationships with them while our teams were working on their homes or properties, we had no way to sustain that initial momentum. Without a framework for regular contact, our clients would be drawn back into isolation and hopelessness through old habits and the conflicting influences of our society.

Once again, I was reminded of those frequent mission trips to south Texas and the transcendent connections we experienced. The construction work we completed wasn't what made the greatest impact on those families. It was our *ongoing presence*. They knew we were in it for the long haul, and they could count on us coming back. Despite the language barrier and our tremendous cultural differences, we formed relationships through our shared bond in Christ.

The continuing commitment is what really cemented those relationships. It underscored the difference between fleeting contact and a lasting connection with the power to break the chains of isolation.

That left me with a big question: How do you infuse "ongoing presence" into the business model of a nonprofit with limited resources?

The reality is, we didn't have the capacity to help every single isolated person in Lake Travis. But we could try to pinpoint the ones with the greatest potential to actually escape the bonds of isolation—those who would be willing to let us serve them with our *ongoing presence.*

This idea snowballed into a radical change for Partners in Hope.

We decided to ask our clients to sign a year-long contract before we would agree to work with them. To say that was an unusual approach is probably a vast understatement.

From the outset, we recognized that some people wouldn't be interested or willing to accept long-term support. We anticipated the push-back. "Let me get this straight… You won't clean up my yard unless I promise to be your friend for a year?" Point taken.

We quickly discovered that the resistance had a predictable theme. People didn't really know what to do with this strange offer or whether they could trust us. That seemed to be a significant roadblock. And yet, we firmly believed this could play a major role in chipping away at the isolation epidemic.

How does it work?

The front part of the process remains the same. People in need still reach out to the community nonprofit or agency best equipped to solve their specific problem. If these groups recognize that the people they're assisting also need help to improve their living conditions, they make the referral to Partners in Hope. Then we reach out to these individuals and offer our assistance.

From there, things are different. Before we begin any work, we explain our long-term operating model.

> *Our team not only provides repairs and clean-up for our clients' homes and properties, but we also walk through a season of life with them and act as a gateway to something much more profound.*

If they agree to an extended partnership with us, we give them access to a network of support over time that helps them reconnect with their neighbors, local churches and their community.

But first, they have to be willing to work with us for at least 12 months— a commitment we make together in a written agreement.

We weren't trying to be legalistic or rigid with the contract. We simply wanted a way to clearly define the agreement as a two-way commitment and provide details about the expectations for our clients and our staff members. This was a whole new ballgame, and nobody really knew the rules. We needed to add some structure.

The more we talked through this arrangement with our potential clients, the more their underlying desire for relationships came out. They really didn't want to go through life's ups and downs all alone. As odd as our proposal might have initially sounded, they were drawn to the idea of having a support system that didn't disappear at the first sign of trouble.

The individuals or families interested in working with Partners in Hope complete an application for our review. We follow up with multiple conversations to ensure that everyone is on the same page with the expectations for our partnership. If all the pieces seem to fit, we ask them to sign our agreement.

The contract confirms the clients' willingness to do the following:

- Maintain a relationship with Partners in Hope that extends for a minimum of 12 months.
- Receive assistance from volunteers (primarily with local churches) to meet their immediate needs for help with living conditions.
- Read *God Will Use This for Good* (a booklet by Max Lucado) and discuss the content with a Partners in Hope staff member.
- Participate in goal-setting by sharing their plans to move forward and allowing Partners in Hope to seek ways to support them in achieving those goals.
- Speak openly about their progress at monthly check-in meetings with a Partners in Hope staff member.
- Participate in regular fellowship events sponsored by Partners in Hope.
- Work with Partners in Hope to find opportunities for engaging with the community to use their unique skills and talents.

What does Partners in Hope offer?

To fulfill our side of the agreement, Partners in Hope takes intentional steps to build positive, long-term relationships with our clients and to reconnect them with their neighbors.

We generally provide support in four different ways:

1. Opportunities for Connection and Fellowship

After our initial contact with potential clients, we discuss with them the possibility of a long-term partnership. If they agree, we call and visit them frequently during the year. These check-ins allow us to get updates on their goals, understand the challenges they are facing, celebrate their wins, provide emotional and spiritual support, and actively look for ways to connect them with helpful people and resources.

In addition, we send them a monthly newsletter with information about opportunities to have fellowship with us and others in their area. Our Sunday Suppers (hosted each month by a local church) bring together our clients, our staff members and community volunteers to enjoy a delicious meal and good conversation. We've also been inviting our female clients to join with other women in their neighborhoods for our weekly Coffee Connection and Bible Study.

2. Home and Property Improvements

Since home-improvement services had been our usual point of entry with new clients, we often kick off this more formal partnership with a team workday at their property. We coordinate local volunteers from area churches and other sources to do the work, with repairs sometimes continuing over the course of several weeks or months. Sometimes specific vendors may be needed, which gives us an opportunity to share our mission with other members of the community. God has used many of these interactions to impact lives we wouldn't have otherwise been able to touch.

3. Personalized Support

As we build relationships with these neighbors in need, we have the unique opportunity to customize the way they can take steps toward greater community. Every client is different. By getting to know them over time, we gain an inside view of their lives that allows us to detect and meet hidden needs that could be holding them back.

For instance, we worked to connect one client with what he needed most at the time: a smoking cessation program. He could only move into an assisted living facility (which was imperative) if he was a non-smoker. Another client desperately needed a certain type of medical equipment, and we connected her with the right resource to get it. And sometimes, the connections we provide fall into a much more personal category.

We were working with a woman named Sabina, who was a single mother with five young children. She was operating and manning a food truck, working as many hours as possible to make ends meet. But every time one of her children needed to be somewhere (a school event, doctor's appointment, extracurricular activity), she'd have to close down the food truck—which meant lost revenue. She was becoming increasingly anxious about her financial situation and parenting logistics.

A critical thing Sabina needed to make her life better was help with transportation. One of her daughters was 15 and would soon be eligible for a driver's license. However, Sabina didn't have the money to send her to a driving school, nor the proper documentation (or the time) to become her driving coach.

Partners in Hope connected Sabina with a number of church volunteers to assist, and some of them stepped in to become driving coaches. They helped the daughter practice so she could get her license. Once the daughter was able to take on more of the drop-off and pick-up duties for the other children, Sabina was able to keep the food truck open more consistently, increasing her income and relieving some of the stress involved with managing her family.

Without being in a relationship with people and learning about their daily challenges, we wouldn't be able to personalize the connections we provide for them.

The key is listening carefully and being resourceful to identify a few simple things that could make an enormous difference in their lives.

4. Household Resource Referrals

While we don't specifically collect or store household items at Partners in Hope, we do try to use them as a bonus opportunity for connections. We often get calls from people in the community who want to donate something—a dryer, a table, a refrigerator—and we can usually think of a client who is in need of that item. But whenever possible, we avoid being the middleman.

We try to coordinate a time when the donor can meet directly with the client to deliver the item and create the potential for another connection. In some cases, relationships have formed from those meetings and, in others, it's a one-time event. Either way, a face-to-face exchange has a greater impact on both parties than an anonymous drop-off.

How do you measure the client impact?

Using this emerging model, we've seen people experience life-altering changes. Granted, it doesn't work with every single client. Sometimes we just can't break through. But when we do succeed, the outcomes have been (in our view) extraordinary.

> *Many of our previously isolated clients have progressed to experience new chapters in their lives—as good neighbors, as part of church families, and as seekers who are growing in their relationships with Christ.*

In the Introduction, I described our efforts to help a woman named Laura. Several years of being disabled and unemployed had left her alone and disconnected from life. This chapter wouldn't be complete without sharing the surprising cascade of love that she created through our partnership.

After our team got to know Laura and spent time working on her property, we watched the joy come back into her life. Those connections were like threads, pulling her back into the community and giving her a new perspective. She had been attending our monthly fellowship dinners, and she made good friends who enjoyed lively conversations just as much as she did.

Several years after we met Laura, she received a long-awaited settlement that would allow her to sell her property in Lake Travis and move back to the city where her family and friends lived. She reached out to share her news and also to ask for my help.

Laura told me that several months earlier she noticed a woman who had fallen in front of her mobile home in their neighborhood. Her name was Phyllis, and Laura stopped to help the woman get back inside. Surprisingly, Phyllis had been living across the street for 20 years, but they never really knew each other.

Phyllis had once been employed at a home improvement store before having a stroke that left her unable to work. Her mobility was severely limited, and she frequently stumbled. Her older brother was living with her and did his best to care for her until he died about a year later.

After that, Phyllis was all alone. She was primarily confined to the trailer, and she could barely get around. Consequently, her mobile home was experiencing severe decay, and the yard she always took pride in keeping tidy was neglected. She couldn't mow the lawn herself, and she rarely had any extra cash to pay someone else to do it.

Laura instantly understood what Phyllis' life was like, because she had lived it herself. She knew about the isolation and the suffering from her own painful past. The two women became friends, but now Laura was moving. She was desperate for Partners in Hope to support Phyllis the same way we had supported her.

> *Laura had personally experienced the value of connection. She knew it saved her life, and she couldn't bear the thought of Phyllis returning to a completely isolated existence.*

We set up a time to go and visit Phyllis together.

As soon as we arrived, I could tell that Laura had set the stage for this relationship. Phyllis greeted us with a cautiously hopeful look. She invited us in and then wobbled precariously toward a nearby chair. I held my breath, wondering if she might fall before she reached it.

The three of us had a great conversation and, with Laura's full endorsement, Phyllis signed our agreement. She didn't quite understand all the specific details, but she was overwhelmed and emotional at the realization that she would no longer be facing life alone.

We pulled together a team of community volunteers to work on her property and began building a relationship with her. Several months later, during one of our scheduled follow-up visits, Phyllis told me that she grew up identifying with a particular religious denomination. When I asked whether she ever visited the local church on the outer edge of her neighborhood, she shyly admitted she'd never noticed it before. She added that she hadn't attended church in more than 40 years.

Right after this conversation, I reached out to someone at the nearby church for help in serving Phyllis, and they were happy to provide some volunteers. A friendly group from the church came out and did some work in the yard. After that, Phyllis took the brave step of visiting the church and periodically attended services there.

One of Phyllis' biggest challenges remained: her unsteady gait and lack of balance. We learned about a program sponsored by the Methodist Healthcare Ministries that was helping people address their mobility issues. Group members, led by our community nurse partner, gathered on Tuesday and Thursday mornings to walk. No sprints, no marathons. Just friends having conversations and walking at a leisurely pace to build their strength and stamina.

We asked the nurse if she would reach out to Phyllis and invite her to join the group. Surprisingly, Phyllis said yes.

She couldn't go very far at first, but her new walking partners didn't seem to mind. They were patient and encouraging, and Phyllis loved the camaraderie. Slowly but surely, as the weeks went by, Phyllis started to regain her strength and her balance. The people in this group became her friends and, in some ways, her lifeline.

The first time I saw Phyllis dressed in her exercise gear, full of enthusiasm and ready to log in those daily steps, I was speechless. I couldn't believe it was the same person who could barely make it to the chair in our initial meeting.

This example demonstrates some of the best parts of our new model focused on connection. Laura, a former client, took the lead in connecting us with Phyllis. We connected Phyllis with volunteers to repair her house. We helped a local church begin a connection with her. We connected Phyllis with supportive friends who helped improve her physical and mental health.

With Phyllis, we saw a life transformed by the power of connection.

How do you measure the community impact?

Another advantage of the new model used by Partners in Hope is the way it naturally produces the most qualified volunteers to help other isolated people in the community.

> *Only those who have experienced the depths of sadness that come with isolation can truly relate to those who are suffering from it.*

Just like Laura, many of our clients inevitably become compassionate, understanding volunteers to serve those who are still stuck in that desolate pit. Their ability to empathize and connect is phenomenal, and they often emerge as vital parts of our team in serving the community.

Seeing that ripple effect of neighbors serving neighbors has been one of the most rewarding parts of this whole process. With each person we help at Partners in Hope, we are effectively increasing the size of our "army" to serve the rest of the community. The sheer enthusiasm for helping others becomes contagious, and it starts to spread through the community like wildfire.

One connection becomes two. Two become four. Four become eight. The number of lives we can impact starts to grow dramatically.

By leveraging the power of ongoing presence as part of our operating model at Partners in Hope, we were doing more than just rescuing people from social isolation and leading them toward the Kingdom of God. We were also creating a powerful, new stream of volunteers to help us in the fight.

In Chapter Two, I shared the story of Audrey who called me for help on the day of her husband's funeral when her homeowners' association was threatening to take action against her. Partners in Hope stepped in to support her, using our new operating model.

Audrey willingly signed the agreement, and she was extremely grateful for our help. At the time, she felt like she was in a horrifying freefall from 30,000 feet, and we were offering her a parachute.

Over the next few months, we coordinated the efforts of multiple community churches and local groups to help clean up her property.

Volunteers brought in wheelbarrows and shovels, and some days we had more than 40 people busily working to remove the remnants of the fire in her shed.

Audrey watched this process in complete amazement, and she was visibly moved by the sight of so many people helping a neighbor in need. For someone who had lived the last part of her life separated from the outside world, she was now soaking in the personal contact. She loved to sit on her front porch and visit with the volunteers, learning about their families and sharing stories of her husband.

As we were finishing one of our workdays, I remember a volunteer approached me with an interesting but not totally unexpected comment. He confidently told me that the work done by teams with dozens of people over multiple weeks could have been done by one guy with a backhoe in a couple of days.

I smiled at him, nodded, and told him he was absolutely correct.

I went on to explain that efficiency wasn't the goal for Partners in Hope. We were focused on building connections and relationships. Because of this lengthy experience, Audrey knew there were dozens of people in her community who cared enough about her to do this back-breaking work. She developed strong friendships with some of the people who showed up, day after day. The volunteers got to know her. They grieved with her and, later, celebrated this new beginning.

Using a backhoe would have quickly left Audrey alone in her now-acceptable yard. The main point was the connection, not the cleaning.

Once the work on her property was finished and the homeowner's association was satisfied, Partners in Hope continued its relationship with Audrey. She became a regular participant at our monthly events, and she was quickly expanding her circle of friends.

Since she was bilingual, Audrey eagerly volunteered to help us communicate with some of the Hispanic families who attended our Sunday Suppers. She was thrilled to become the "resident translator," and we watched her warm, welcoming demeanor begin to blossom.

Audrey also began attending a Methodist church located fairly close to her neighborhood.

Inspired by the support she received at such a low time in her life, she adopted a real mindset of ministry and frequently served others in her neighborhood.

Everyone could see that Audrey's outlook on life was remarkably different than the day we first met. She emerged from feeling hopeless and alone to being hopeful and optimistic, ready to share in loving others and supporting them when life gets rough.

It was a beautiful thing to witness. And we knew it wouldn't have happened if one man with a backhoe dropped by on a weekend to clean up her property. Ongoing presence really was the "secret sauce" in our model.

What happens when the contract expires?

Audrey's transformation actually spanned more than three years, and she still attends our events. From that angle, I want to point out that the 12-month agreement is more symbolic than specific. We're trying to help people create a habit of regular connection as a long-term answer to the isolation problem. If they hang in there for 365 days, they usually want to keep going—and we're there for them.

Ideally, our contracts turn into actual relationships, and we've been blessed to see that happen many times. In fact, some of our clients have been involved with Partners in Hope for more than eight years now.

What does this emerging model look like?

In some ways, any type of graphic depiction of this model is a bit misleading. The process is never the same twice, and it rarely occurs in a neat, orderly fashion. With that said, there's still an advantage to defining the typical order of intentional steps we follow and illustrating it in an idealized manner. The steps in the process include:

- Make the initial contact and build trust.
- Establish a 12-month partnership using a contract.
- Link the client to local resources and support.
- Meet an immediate living-condition need.
- Intentionally connect churches to the client.
- Invite the client to regular fellowship events.
- Build the relationship over time with personalized support.
- Provide opportunities for the client to engage with the community.

- Pursue the client to become part of the body of Christ throughout the journey.

In a perfect world, we guide isolated people through these steps and into a circle of community with a process that, generally speaking, looks like this:

The Serving Model
Partners in Hope

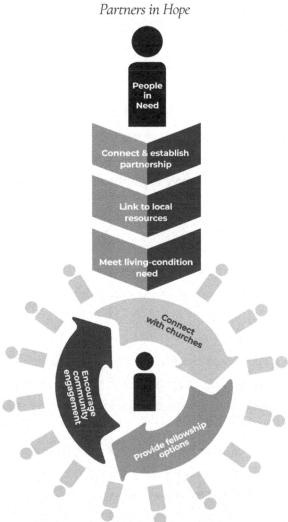

Now for the obvious "fine print": *We don't live in a perfect world.*

In some cases, clients who have been with us for many months reach out with another urgent need. Initially we might have repaired a fence, but they ask for help again when the heater breaks in the winter. They know someone has their back in a crisis, and this is another way we get to serve them with our ongoing presence.

Other clients get stalled or never make it to the circle of community. The point is, this isn't usually a linear process but more of a dynamic flow with some twists and turns.

Throughout my time with Partners in Hope, people have often asked me about measuring the effectiveness of our model. Do you have any statistics about your impact? How long does it take to move one person from isolation to community? Is there a quantifiable formula we *can* replicate for success?

These are certainly valid questions, and it really frustrates me that I can't produce a fancy spreadsheet to document the "return on investment" for each client. Ministry just doesn't work that way. But here's what I can tell you.

The serving model I've shown you depicts one person going through the process. Now that we've been applying that model in some form for more than 10 years, we're seeing some results that we can't even take credit for.

Since every client we serve becomes part of the flow toward community, we like to think of the collective, long-term process as a river. Partners in Hope takes intentional steps to facilitate connections, bringing more and more clients and qualified volunteers into the river over time. The results of our efforts are significantly amplified when these community volunteers are better prepared to interact with others and proactive about making connections beyond the scope of our services.

The Ripple Effect

How the Serving Process Impacts the Community

The Problem: Isolation

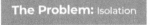

Flow:
From stagnant water of isolation to living water of loving community

Ripples:
Indications of flow downstream where relationships develop outside of planned activities

Intentional Actions Create Flow:

- Home Improvement
- Small Groups
- Sunday Suppers
- Meal Delivery
- Volunteer Equipping
- Ongoing Response to Needs

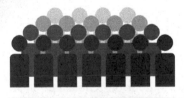

The VIsion:
A community empowered to work together to eliminate hopelessness and isolation

The further downstream those connections happen, the harder it is to trace them back to our direct involvement. That's when we get to see God at work, creating cumulative ripple effects that only He could orchestrate. After more than a decade of work, God has opened our eyes to see not only individual change but also widespread community impact that we never could have planned.

Sometimes weeks, months or even years later, we'll hear a story about personal connections that had transformative power for our clients—and many times, we weren't even involved in facilitating those relationships.

I remember sitting at a table during one of our Sunday Suppers with a client and a volunteer who was a member of a church that had hosted the dinner three months earlier. As I listened to their animated conversation, I discovered they had developed a friendship and were getting together regularly for coffee and Bible study.

On their own, many of our clients have brought more people into the flow downstream as they became more engaged with the community. Audrey, for instance, began actively serving others in her neighborhood and built loving relationships that opened the door for her to share what God had done in her life.

Without our client Laura, we never would have met Phyllis. Just a few weeks ago, I got a call from a leader at Phyllis' church. She wanted to let me know that Phyllis had been hospitalized with a cracked vertebrae. Not wanting her to go through that alone, I jumped in my car and headed straight to the hospital. I walked down the hall, past the nurses' station, and knocked on the door. What I saw when I walked inside completely caught me off guard.

Despite the pain she was likely experiencing, Phyllis was surprisingly cheerful and greeted me with a big smile. She said she'd been busy with visits and phone calls from many of her church friends and walking buddies. They had been checking on her and were ready to help with whatever she needed once she was released to go home.

Phyllis made many of these connections without our assistance. Now these people were graciously surrounding her in God's love and sustaining her during this tough time. She could feel it. And I could see it in her face.

No, we can't calculate the exact impact of our work in this lifetime, but God is sending us a loud and clear message. If we faithfully do what He's asked of us, he'll take care of it from there.

The ripples of connection are happening. They are real. And they are glorious.

CHAPTER FIVE

THE NETWORK

Sometimes God's love looks like a children's swing set.
Sometimes it looks like a set of dentures. Who knew?

We can do the most good for the Kingdom of God if all the parts of the Kingdom work together.

While the last chapter provided an up-close look at our relationships with our clients, this one will present a wide-angled view of our connections with the community organizations that share our mission to serve neighbors in need, including local churches and other faith-based nonprofits.

For our new Partners in Hope model to be successful and scalable, we had to get more people involved with our clients over a longer period of time. That would require tapping into other resources throughout Lake Travis in ways we hadn't previously done.

> *Oddly enough, it seemed like the theme of connection that was driving our efforts to serve isolated people might also apply to our interactions with other community organizations.*

Did we have a grand vision for how to achieve our goals? No. At least not at the beginning. We were, once again, flying into all-new territory—and grateful to know that God was our navigator.

At the time, we simply set out to implement our updated operating model by connecting our clients to more resources and volunteers. We never expected that process to reveal something profound. Something radical. Something we wouldn't understand until after the fact.

In the next few sections, I'll tell you about some of our experiences teaming up with different organizations throughout the community as we sought to create more meaningful connections for our clients.

Partnering with Other Nonprofits

1. A Reason to Smile

Throughout my years with Partners in Hope, I frequently worked with the people at Lake Travis Crisis Ministries and developed a good rapport with them. I tried to be deliberate with my presence at their office, typically visiting on a weekly basis. While I was there, I met with staff members to let them know about our work and asked them to keep us in mind if they had clients in need of home or property repair—things that would let us connect volunteers at their homes.

The Crisis Ministries staff often gave us referrals and, occasionally, introduced me to a client while I was on site. If we started working with one of their clients, we were diligent about giving the staff updates and keeping them informed about our progress. We also sent them referrals as we found people who could use their assistance.

As time went by, the collaboration between our organizations really seemed to blossom. Crisis Ministries committed to reimburse us for some of the expenses related to home-repair materials used for our common clients. They even agreed to work with certain people who lived outside their normal geographic area if Partners in Hope was involved.

This relationship played an important role in our work with a woman named Janice. She was referred to us through a local church and was facing a number of difficulties in her life. Besides having one prosthetic leg, she desperately needed a hip replacement. She was already having trouble getting up the steps to her trailer, so she was understandably anxious about how to manage that right after major surgery.

With that in mind, our first workday for Janice involved building a ramp that would help her get inside the trailer despite her limited mobility. We also replaced some flooring inside and added a new coat of paint to several rooms. Helpful adjustments, of course. But we also came to the realization that those repairs still wouldn't give Janice the confidence she needed to fully reintegrate into the community.

Why? Her teeth.

Most of them were missing, and the rest were in terrible shape. I couldn't imagine how this made her feel, but I knew it probably fed her insecurity. At one point, Janice even shared with me that she had been trying to save money for a long time to get a full set of dentures.

Knowing that Crisis Ministries had a connection with a local dentist who offered a discount to their clients, I contacted the organization to see if they might consider adding Janice to their roster. They agreed, and the dentist promptly provided an estimate for completing Janice's dental work. Although he offered a substantial discount, the cost was still prohibitive. We needed a creative solution.

After Crisis Ministries graciously offered to pay a portion of that expense, we reached out to the church that originally told us about Janice. We explained the situation and asked if they might be willing to split the remainder of the cost with Partners in Hope. We were delighted when they said yes.

All along, I had encouraged Janice to pray that God would work it out and provide. Making the call to tell her the good news about the funding was definitely one of the cool moments that I am blessed to get to experience in my role.

I remember when Janice came to see me the first time after receiving her dentures. She was absolutely beaming. She had always impressed me as a positive person—someone who cared for others even while she was facing her own trials. We were thrilled that this blessing could happen for her, and we knew she would somehow use it to show love to others. Sure enough, Janice became one of our greatest ambassadors.

While I always found it deeply gratifying to watch team members combine their efforts for mission activities, this was something different.

God was now showing me the power of teamwork on a monumentally bigger scale. Beyond the church. Across the nonprofit sector. Throughout the community.

That was an interesting clue for things to come.

2. Home is Where the Heart is

In another instance, we received a call from a nonprofit ministry called Helping Hands, which was located near Lake Travis in the Spicewood area. This organization operated a transitional home for families who needed temporary housing due to difficult life circumstances. Helping Hands would allow them to stay in this home rent-free for 6-12 months while they got back on their feet.

The leaders at Helping Hands wanted to know if Partners in Hope would consider making some improvements to this home and the surrounding property. While the request was outside the normal scope of our model, we thought it might offer an interesting way to connect with the struggling families who were staying in the home. Perhaps these people would be open to a relationship with us.

Before we got started, we met with the family living at the house, which was a young couple who had two small boys. My initial discussions with the husband were a little tense. I offered to pray with him at one point, and he flat-out refused. His family had been through some dire situations, leaving him mad at the world and angry with God.

Once our team was working on the projects requested by Helping Hands, we did eventually get to know the family on a more personal level. In fact, we recognized an opportunity to further enhance the property while also enhancing their lives. Much to the delight of the children, we built a playscape in the yard behind the house.

A year later, Helping Hands asked for our assistance with the home again—this time with kitchen and deck repairs. A similar occurrence took place during my first meeting with the father of the family currently living there. He didn't object to my prayer, but he made it clear that he was agnostic and said he hoped that wasn't a deal-breaker.

This couple truly wanted help, and they understood social isolation all too well. After losing their jobs and their home, they felt like they had lost their dignity. The shame of that situation prompted them to distance themselves from all the people in their lives. They were embarrassed for anyone to see their downfall, telling me many times, "This isn't who we really are."

> *In each of these cases, we were able to make emotional connections with families that didn't have a relationship with God and, at some level, had closed that door.*

I'm happy to report they both eventually became clients with Partners in Hope.

Through our relationships with them, those families are now taking steps toward faith. Their children have attended Vacation Bible School. And we have prayed countless times with those young families—the same ones who once would have never asked us to. How cool is it to see God work in peoples' lives like that?

We have learned that it takes time and almost never works according to our schedule. But we knew our role was to keep showing up, try to consistently demonstrate the love of Jesus, and prove to people we aren't going anywhere. That is what creates the fertile ground God needs to perform His miracles.

3. Just What the Doctor Ordered

Many of the people we serve are facing medical challenges, as well as the added burden of trying to navigate the healthcare system and complicated government support programs. Partners in Hope certainly wasn't an expert in that area, and I knew it would be helpful to have a contact who was.

We heard that the Methodist Healthcare Ministries employed a nurse named Melanie who officed out of a local church. I decided to reach out to tell her about Partners in Hope and talk about how we might work together. After I introduced myself and began to explain why I was calling, there was a long silence. She was...speechless. And then she laughed.

Seconds before she took my call, she had been on the phone with her supervisor who explained a new directive for all of the satellite nurses to participate in more community programs. Melanie barely had a moment to think "how in the world am I going to do that?" before my call answered the question. Talk about perfect timing.

Melanie was excited about the opportunity to team up with Partners in Hope, and we invited her to join us when we visited some of our clients. She rapidly became a priceless resource for them, and we were extremely grateful to have access to someone with her healthcare background.

After we worked with Melanie for about two years, Partners in Hope began making monthly contributions to the operating budget she used for supporting clients with medical needs. We weren't able to donate a huge amount, but it was huge in Melanie's eyes.

Beyond allowing her to improve the care she gave her patients, the commitment also demonstrated how much we value our partnership with her.

And when her department recently gave her some substantial resources for community service, she immediately contacted us to talk about ways we could collectively utilize the funds.

At one point, we noticed that many of our clients needed support to quit smoking, so we talked with Melanie about this need. Smoking was apparently a common habit among isolated people, and it added to the destructive lifestyle. Melanie was excited to pull together some resources to help those struggling with that challenge.

One month later, we promoted a smoking cessation class to our clients. Initially, three women began meeting with Melanie to work on letting go of this health-eroding addiction. The participants formed a strong and coherent support group, with Melanie coaching them through the whole process. Working together with Melanie, we found a meaningful way to serve our clients with additional connections that improved their well-being.

Partnering with Churches

1. Come to the Table

Several of the regular volunteers with Lake Travis Crisis Ministries were also members of one of the oldest churches in Lake Travis, which created a natural connection for Partners in Hope. The people were already familiar with some of our clients, and we knew they had a real heart for serving their neighbors in need. When we scheduled a workday nearby, these church members were always eager to show up and help.

This church also offered to host some of our Sunday Supper fellowships, and we soon discovered they excelled in this area. Now I can probably guess what you're thinking. What church *can't* pull together a killer potluck? Where there are people worshipping God, there's fellowship. And where there's fellowship, there's food. It's some kind of universal church policy, right? The Lord's people have this down to a science.

My response? Well, sort of. When we first started our Sunday Suppers, members of the different hosting churches kindly prepared and served the meals—but then they tended to watch the rest from the kitchen. It took some time for us to change the mentality around that.

> *We wanted the evening to be less about being fed and more about feeding on God's love together.*

This long-established church totally "got it." They provided delicious food but, more importantly, they were comfortable sharing the experience. Sitting at the table with all types of people. Eating together. Engaging with our clients and listening to their stories. Praying with them and loving on them. Those wonderful evenings were just as fulfilling for the church members as they were for our clients.

The partnership with this church deepened when the pastor told me they would love to be our stand-by hosts for Sunday Suppers any time we couldn't find another congregation to volunteer. That was a huge relief, knowing we had some back-up.

Even better, we started to see that our connection with this church was drawing people into their ministry programs. A couple of our clients started participating in their Men's Bible Study, and several actually joined the church.

In one instance, we invited two of our brand new clients to a Sunday Supper held in their fellowship hall. This couple had been distant from church for most of their marriage, but they had a new urgency to reconnect: the husband's fight against cancer. The pastor and I collaborated to get care for him over the next six months. When he passed, we jointly officiated the funeral.

Four weeks later, his wife was also tragically diagnosed with cancer. We continued ministering to her family and building relationships during this extremely difficult season of life. Almost exactly one year later, we had the privilege of co-officiating her funeral as well.

Throughout the sad journey, the couple told us on many occasions how much it meant to have the combined support of Partners in Hope and a loving church family. Honestly, the most powerful thing we did was to connect them with a church. Not just any church—THEIR church. Those relationships within that congregation deeply changed the 18 painful months before they were reunited in Heaven. That really sunk in for me. I had a role to play, and it was connecting them to the Kingdom.

2. Skip the Projects, Serve the People

Since I had met a number of people who attended a large church in the Lake Travis area, I reached out regularly to that congregation for 3-4 years to see how we might collaborate in serving those in need. This potential partnership seemed like a great fit, since the church had an established ministry that provided help with home improvement. This fairly large group of men (with a significant number of power tools) routinely did repair work, construction and disaster relief.

Early on, the men's work project group participated with several of the Partners in Hope workdays and lent their considerable skills to our efforts. However, their availability was somewhat limited. Their church became very involved with developing a new community to support the homeless population, and that endeavor emerged as a primary focus for the men's work project team.

Since the group members were frequently busy, they encouraged me to pursue other opportunities with the church. I reached out to the pastors, the leaders for Men's and Women's Adult Ministries, even the Youth Minister, all with hopes of making some connections. What I found there—and what occurs in many large, established churches—was a highly organized hierarchy of structure. Each ministry segment was led by a staff member who was responsible for decision-making in that area. In other words, the structure created a silo effect even within the church.

Each time I identified an opportunity to team up with a certain group in the church, I was ultimately referred back to the men's work project team.

I likely wasn't following the usual pattern of partnership they had experienced with other nonprofits in the past, and I could tell they didn't really know what to do with me.

No matter what I did, I kept ending up at the same place. But then several things happened.

The church added a new staff member named Curt, who was in charge of local missions. He was evaluating all of the current mission activities and exploring opportunities to try something new. I was delighted when he invited me to tell him more about Partners in Hope. About the same time, the construction and development at the homeless community were wrapping up, so the men's work group was looking for new opportunities.

Shortly after my meeting with Curt, I got a call from him. He wanted to know if Partners in Hope might be able to help with one of their church members who was experiencing a crisis.

He explained that this woman was struggling to care for two disabled adult children, and her husband was in prison with a trial under way. The wife was concerned about her safety and that of her children if he were to be released. In the meantime, her trailer was in serious need of help.

I knew the woman lived just outside of our usual geographic area for Lake Travis, but this seemed like a perfect opportunity to kick off a stronger relationship with the church—one I'd been trying to forge for quite some time. I told Curt that I'd be willing to help coordinate the services, but I would need access to more church ministries and volunteers to implement our full model of connection. He was completely on board.

After all the attempts, a true partnership with this church emerged when we joined forces to serve a family together. Collectively.

As a team, we figured out the best way to provide support for this family as their circumstances changed over time. That's a very different approach than looking at ministry as a project-based activity to meet a specific need. The client was the focus. Relationships and connections made it possible.

In my eyes, the biggest breakthrough is what happened next. The partnership experience with this church has really grown deeper since our initial serving collaboration. We are now teaming up to minister to another family in the area, and the church also hosted one of our Sunday Suppers for the very first time. I'd spent so many years trying to develop that connection, and I was humbled to see the relationship come to fruition. Today, we are poised for the partnership to continue growing.

3. Front-Yard Fellowship

Partners in Hope became connected with a newer church when one of the pastors there reached out to ask if we might facilitate a serving opportunity for the members of its youth group. They were celebrating a special missions week and wanted to get the kids involved with helping someone in the community.

As I was trying to think about which of our clients could use some help around the house, I immediately thought of Tori. She was a single mom of three, and Partners in Hope had been walking with her on her journey for about six months and doing repairs on her home.

During one of our meetings, Tori mentioned how much she loved children. Always had. She told me she worried about some of the neighborhood kids who seemed to spend a significant amount of time out on their own. Tori would often invite them to come play games in the yard with her own children, and she usually had some snacks on hand to share.

The wheels in my brain started to turn. What if we asked Tori to host a Backyard Bible Club for the neighborhood children? We could connect her with the members of the youth group to plan, organize and run the event. This was quite a departure from the workday we originally envisioned, but I thought it might be just the right fit.

Luckily, Tori and the youth pastor did, too. They were both thrilled about the idea. After selecting the days to hold the Bible Club, Tori met with members of the youth group to plan the lessons and activities, create promotional flyers, and distribute them around the blocks near her home.

On the three days of the event (which, by the way, we held in her front yard), the youth pastor and six youth group members from the church welcomed more than a dozen neighborhood children. Tori participated as the kids interacted, talking about the Bible and playing games. The laughter was good for her soul.

From our viewpoint, the connections that took place on those days were amazing. Partners in Hope teamed up with a wonderful church to serve a client, opening the door for future collaboration. Tori got to know the pastor and other church members in the process, increasing the chances she might attend their services or encourage her children to get involved with the youth group. And the church found a creative way to meet more people right in their own back yard.

That was an important step in what has become a thriving partnership with this local church.

> *Out-of-the-box thinking and unexpected collaboration delivered positive outcomes for everyone involved.*

Finding the Meaning

Even in the absence of a detailed strategy to implement our model, Partners in Hope was getting some exciting results. Whatever we were doing appeared to be working! With the benefit of our "success stories," it was time to analyze the process and more carefully define it so we could make it repeatable.

Several insights emerged at that point.

First, every client interaction was different. All of them had different backstories, challenges, and circumstances. In other words, supporting them wasn't a generic, one-size-fits-all event.

> *Using our signature ingredient of ongoing presence to walk with these clients over a period of time, we got to know them well enough to spot unique, hidden opportunities for service that might have otherwise been overlooked.*

Yes, we started the process with home and property repairs, but the life-changing acts of service that followed often came in very different forms.

For Janice, it was new dentures. For Sabina, it was help for her daughter to get a driver's license. For Phyllis, it was supportive friends who helped her regain her health. Hammers and nails definitely took a backseat.

Second, we had been intensely focused on creating more meaningful connections for our clients. At the time, everything else was kind of a blur.

In retrospect, our connection-building process was really unconventional. We had basically been ignoring the usual silos and the standard operating procedures for community service. If one of our clients had a need, we contacted the best organization to help with that.

Sometimes that was a fellow nonprofit ministry with an area of specialization. And sometimes that was a local church whose members were enthusiastic about sharing certain skills and talents. We selectively chose to make connections with the partners who could give our clients the greatest potential for success and the greatest opportunities for connecting with a local church. In the process, we threw the unwritten rules of engagement right out the window. Not on purpose, but that's how it unfolded.

I must admit, my constant conversations about the importance of relationships probably got a little annoying. But for the most part, our fellow community organizations and local churches were open to our innovative partnerships and welcomed a different approach.

With every one of these encounters—these customized, rule-breaking collaborations—we could see an infinitely greater impact on the lives of our clients. We watched in awe as they became part of the community and part of church families. The pieces of the puzzle were falling into place. Although we couldn't visualize it in advance, the after-the-fact clarity was startling.

God was challenging us to "rewire" the community for serving people in need.

We were as surprised as anyone to realize that helping isolated people was just the tip of the iceberg. The Lord seemed to be telling us that our broader objective was to mobilize the Kingdom within our community to participate in the process.

The truth is, churches and faith-based nonprofits have a shared Kingdom goal. Sometimes that potential synergy is neglected because nonprofits also have concrete, interim objectives. Feeding hungry people. Helping the unemployed find jobs. Providing support for those with mental illness. But, at the end of the day, they are still nonprofit *ministries*. Just like the churches down the street, they want to bring more people in to the body of Christ.

From that perspective, it didn't make sense for churches and nonprofit ministries to continue playing on different fields while trying to win the same game. Somehow we needed to inspire more of them to move out of their natural silos and form a network that would help us sustain the momentum of the relationships we were developing.

Calculating the Results

As we worked to create dynamic, cross-functional partnerships through-out the Lake Travis area, the far-reaching impact of these connections began to appear.

- We were connecting local churches through unique part-nerships to consistently walk with our clients through tough seasons of life.
- We were learning how to help nonprofit ministries redefine their relationships with local churches as long-term, cooperative affiliations.
- We were helping churches reach out to their neighbors in different ways, giving them new tools to become more visible and approachable.
- We were opening the door for more families to get involved with local churches.
- We were creating a stronger link between church members and their mission activities, encouraging greater participation from enthusiastic, better-prepared volunteers.
- We were building relationships with isolated people to help connect them with the community, with a church family, and with the Kingdom of God.

Changing the Paradigm

With the benefit of these new insights and the value of our connections, we needed to make some strategic changes. On the top of the list was a shift to elevate our organization's vision statement.

> *Partners in Hope will empower the Lake Travis community to work together to eliminate hopelessness and isolation.*

Next up? We needed to reimagine the community serving paradigm as one that served the Kingdom to better reflect God's lofty challenge. Remember the traditional process from Chapter Three?

We had seen the advantage of replacing the silos and separation with collaboration and communication. And in those instances when we got all the parts of the Kingdom to work together, we saw something extraordinary. It was a powerful network moving together toward a common Kingdom goal: *to rescue our isolated neighbors, intentionally draw them into local church families, and welcome them into the body of Christ.*

Ideally, that shift from old paradigm to new paradigm would look something like this:

Traditional Serving Paradigm

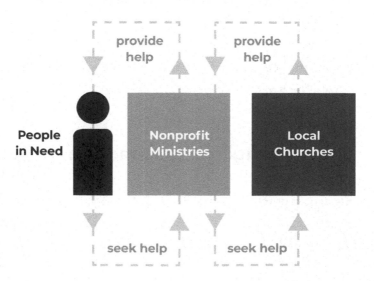

Kingdom Serving Paradigm

In Chapter Eight, I'll talk more about this Kingdom Serving Paradigm and provide details about how you can begin implementing it.

Impacting the Kingdom

OK, this is it. This is the section I want you to remember long after you've finished reading this book.

Partners in Hope embarked on a journey to serve isolated people in the community. We felt called to find solutions to help meet their needs.

In reality, our highest calling was to help the church *become* the solution.

Definitely not our original plan…but so much better!

> *By guiding us to make unexpected connections between local churches, faith-based nonprofits and people in the community, God was giving us some unparalleled tools to make a much bigger impact on the Kingdom.*

It took more than a decade and a willingness to work in some norm-busting, rule-breaking ways. But now we have seen a stunning glimpse of what God had in mind—simultaneously fighting social isolation *and* growing the Kingdom.

In 21st-century vernacular, we might describe that with the popular (although perhaps overused) statement, "Teamwork makes the dream work."

The Apostle Paul essentially told us the same thing thousands of years ago: *We can do the most good for the Kingdom of God if all the parts of the Kingdom work together.*

CHAPTER SIX

THE LESSONS

I'm pretty sure we still have a lot to learn.
And you can bet there will be pop quizzes.

———————————✦———————————

Our entire journey at Partners in Hope has been an experience in on-the-job learning. Every time God revealed another piece of the plan, we had to shift gears and rethink our direction or our methods. That transformational process continues today, as we adjust our model for serving clients to account for global health concerns and economic volatility. Only the Lord knows what's next. Frankly, we might always be a work in progress. And that's OK.

I'm the first to admit that we've made mistakes along the way. In fact, I'm certain we aren't even aware of all the errors and missteps involved, but the lessons we've learned have been infinitely valuable. In this chapter, I want to share some of those with you.

1. Social isolation stems from chronic issues, not a crisis.

In refining the way we serve, we learned how to look at the larger category of "people in need" and identify those who are actually suffering from social isolation. That became a distinguishing aspect of our ministry—doing restorative work with people in chronic circumstances, instead of doing relief work with those in crisis situations.

Every community will have its fair share of people who are experiencing a crisis. I'm referring to a devastating, one-time event that knocks them to their knees. Maybe that's a flood, a fire, a cancer diagnosis, the untimely death of a child. The pain is very real for them, and they may require community resources to make a comeback. But, thankfully, many of them also have friends and family members who are able and willing to help them crawl out of this temporary hole.

Crisis situations also have a way of generating wider community support. There's a tangible event that grabs attention, usually followed by news coverage and social media buzz. If a tornado wipes out all the homes on one block of a neighborhood, heavy-hitting resources such as the American Red Cross or Austin Disaster Relief Network are deployed to lead the response.

In these types of circumstances, the crisis appears to be more of a contained event with a defined recovery objective. There's a start date (when the tornado hit) and an end date (when the families move back into new homes). While the emotional impact of the trauma could linger for years, the crisis response is still primarily viewed in terms of the clear physical needs.

The general public can easily understand these problems, and they are more inclined to help—either pitching in to remove debris, providing meals for first responders, or contributing to the GoFundMe pages that benefit the affected families.

In contrast, social isolation is a chronic condition that involves a progressive domino effect of tragedies that fall in slow motion over months, years or even decades.

Less publicly noticeable situations just pile up, one after the other, eventually becoming a crushing weight to the spirit of the person trapped underneath. Abuse. Divorce. Addiction. Disease. Unemployment. Depression. Homelessness.

And here's the most critical part. Without a support network, they have no one in their lives who can offer help. They end up hiding all alone below the heavy weight of bad luck or bad choices, and hopelessness sets in. While most of us can deal with one big challenge at a time, the cumulative effect of multiple setbacks with no support is what pulls them under water.

> *Chronic conditions are also much more difficult for community members to grasp—and to solve.*

The problems don't have precise boundaries. No start and finish dates. Just open-ended timelines with much bigger challenges and no apparent solutions. That explains why "helpers" get frustrated when responding to chronic issues such as social isolation. It's not easy, and there are a lot of unknowns.

Partners in Hope had to get really comfortable with that kind of uncertainty.

Once we dedicated ourselves to serving socially isolated people, we intentionally looked for those who had chronic, long-term issues and no support system in place. We knew up front that home repair and yard clean-up would *not* solve the problem, but instead be an entry point to offer ongoing support. We made the commitment to walk with them on their extended, often-complicated journeys and help bring new relationships into their lives.

Definitely not the path of least resistance, but a necessary road to travel if we had any hope of making a difference.

2. The key to success lies in the power of "with."

The prevailing theme for Partners in Hope has become ever increasingly about relationships, connections and ongoing presence. To put it another way, we tap into the power of "with."

As strange as this might sound, I really can't adequately describe how much that differentiates the work we do. Even after writing a whole book about it!

Here's why. Our culture conditions us to think about helping others with a fix-it, project-based mentality. We see the need. We meet the need. We move on. That's just the standard process for people serving and the standard expectation for people being served.

Partners in Hope learned that God was giving us a new playbook.

We don't drop off help at the front door; we team up WITH our clients to find the help they need.

It's a long-term approach—and it's not always successful. In fact, the process rarely goes exactly as planned. But we've seen God respond enough times to confirm that "with" is the way He wants us to work. Being in relationships with each other not only allows us to solve specific problems, but it's also the result He wants for all of us.

I never get tired of seeing the pleasantly shocked reaction on the faces of potential clients when we explain that our offer of assistance includes long-term involvement rather than a one-time transaction. Telling someone you want to be in a relationship with them gets a lot of interesting reactions—from completely baffled to openly suspicious to…"who are you?"

Can you imagine a stranger seriously asking you to form a personal partnership? That concept is hard enough to convey in our initial conversations, but it's even harder when using a translator. I can only imagine what some of our Hispanic families must have been thinking when we made that suggestion in a different language. People they've just met are volunteering to walk alongside them, no matter what the future brings. It's completely unexpected.

Despite the many barriers, we can often detect the exact moment when they first understand this will be an actual relationship, not a rescue attempt. That realization is startling and sometimes opens the flood gates of emotion. We've seen quite a few people break down in tears at that point during an initial meeting.

The idea of not being all alone in life plants a tiny seed of hope. As we build trust with each contact and visit, that seed begins to grow. It's a long process, but it takes an extended period of time to reverse a descent into isolation that was likely years in the making.

> *Walking through life with people allows*
> *God to work in His timing.*

We can't be sure when a person's heart will suddenly be opened to God's Spirit. But if we establish trust, show that we care, demonstrate our loyalty even in hard times, and prove we value the relationships, we are perfectly positioned for God to use us according to His plan.

We also learned that the power of "with" applies to more than just our clients. God works to change the hearts of the people who walk beside those suffering from isolation—Partners in Hope staff members, teams from other nonprofits, and church volunteers. The experiences we have in ministering to people in need changes our lives as well. We frequently hear stories about lives that have been touched by the selfless act of giving.

> *God's whole design of serving is less about eliminating needs and more about shaping hearts.*

Jesus made a point of telling us that poor people would always exist. That's not because God can't solve the problem of poverty, but it's to transform the hearts of those who care, share, give, and love. We don't give generously to see how much can be given, but to become givers.

The power of "with" makes all of that possible.

3. Kingdom partnerships between nonprofits and churches create incredible synergy.

As you know from our story, the power of "with" ended up being about much more than just our client relationships. It also became the defining characteristic of our new approach to translate community service into Kingdom building. Working with other nonprofits. Working with local churches. Working with volunteers throughout the community.

This lesson features one of the most stunning discoveries we made along our journey.

> *When nonprofits and churches team up for Kingdom partnerships, the potential for Kingdom impact is virtually limitless.*

With that said, organizations need to approach these partnerships as an investment, not a short-term trial. Many people see the genius in the idea, but they get discouraged when they hit bumps in the road. Trust me, there *will* be some kinks to work out. This is new territory for everyone, but it's worth the effort.

In many cases, partners might want to help but they have no idea how to do it. The learning curve is real. We had to start trying—and keep trying—even when the other groups involved weren't quite sure about the process. Our goal was to be patient. To build trust. To learn about their strengths, passions, and limitations. Each day, we'd watch for God to deliver the right opportunity for us to take a bigger step.

When churches and nonprofits are willing to invest in these long-term relationships, they will reap the benefits of ongoing collaboration and a new breed of collective discipleship that would never have been possible before.

4. *Church members and volunteers are typically unprepared for relational ministry.*

As we moved toward our new vision for a Kingdom Serving Paradigm, we discovered it was a good-news, bad-news scenario.

The good news? Collapsing those silos put more church volunteers on the front lines of mission work to serve those in need, and the collaborative efforts of Kingdom organizations were directing more people toward the church.

The bad news? Members of local congregations don't always have the experience or training to effectively serve people suffering from social isolation, and they may lack the self-confidence to try. They aren't necessarily prepared to go out and pursue them. And they may not know how to welcome and receive them into their church families.

Let's start from the angle of receiving them. Imagine that a person suffering from social isolation shows up for the 11:00 service. What happens?

To be candid, many people in situations of need may not look, sound or have similar mannerisms as the typical members of the church. Their interpersonal skills are likely to be different than what others may expect in that social setting. When members of the congregation unconsciously recognize those disconnects, they may not know how to interact or respond. All of that awkwardness on both sides can leave everyone with a less-than-optimal first impression.

Even though church members have heard countless sermons about loving their neighbors and carrying each other's burdens, those are tough principles to translate when it concerns people with whom they believe they have nothing in common. Inadvertently, they might project unwelcome body language, provide awkward responses to questions or completely avoid them.

This isn't intended as a criticism of the church, but it's a call to acknowledge a problem we need to address. The silo approach historically kept church members at a distance, so they had very limited experience working directly with neighbors in need. They hadn't been exposed to people in these situations, especially in the lobbies of their own churches. They simply didn't understand the circumstances and challenges some people were facing.

There are a lot of valid reasons why church members aren't prepared to welcome and receive people who don't fit the mold. But putting all of that aside, here's the problem. It takes an enormous amount of courage for hopeless, isolated people to visit a church for the first time. If they have a negative experience or just get the impression that they're viewed as outsiders, the chances of them trying again are extremely low.

> *Churches can't take the risk of blowing those one-time opportunities, and members need to be prepared long before someone "different" walks in the door.*

That means church leadership teams should proactively educate members about how to handle those situations with compassion and sensitivity.

Now for the other side of the coin: equipping church members to *pursue* isolated people through mission activities.

Churches are missing an opportunity if they just train their congregations to be ready for whomever comes through the door. The bigger issue is preparing members to go out into the community to meet people where they are.

To serve them, love them, and walk with them in their environment. That's a completely different challenge.

I knew this obstacle had to be removed if we were to collectively push toward our ultimate goal of bringing more people into the Kingdom. I was at a bit of a loss for how to do that, but I knew our model would never be successful if I didn't start somewhere to solve this foundational problem.

In response, I developed a volunteer training program and started reaching out to our local church partners with a request to present the information to their members. That was a tougher sell than you might think.

Originally, I planned to do a one-hour interactive training at a neutral location and invite volunteers from multiple churches to attend. But when I had seen other groups try that sort of thing, the attendees were often the same every time. In general, 10% of church members consistently respond and participate in whatever activity is offered. I wanted to reach the other 90%.

I started asking individual churches if I could come speak to their members on their own turf, at regularly scheduled events or meetings. Small group gatherings. Women's Bible Study sessions. Whatever they had. It took time, persistence and multiple requests but, finally, that approach gained traction.

The key points I discuss during the "Walking with Others" training include the following:

- Be proactive about connections and open to relationships.
- Focus on people, not on projects.
- Listen and be willing to learn.
- Remember you're not providing a solution, but walking with them through the process.
- Know your boundaries.
- Refuel so you have enough energy to pour into others.
- Pray often and let God reveal your intended role in these lives.

That last point is critical, as you might imagine. As we walk, listen, and learn through this experience, we always seek to find the role God wants us to play with a particular person.

Do I have a certain skill or resource that could help them? Am I supposed to connect them to someone else? Can I encourage them or equip them to do something new? We don't (and can't) try to solve all their problems, but we do try to discern what God wants from us while representing Him in each relationship.

I have generally found that the people who participate in these training classes are eager to learn and appreciate the advance guidance.

> *Slowly but surely, we are equipping church members to handle these new situations and welcome relationships they might not have otherwise considered.*

After some years of implementing our new model and working toward the ideal serving paradigm for the community, I continue searching for additional opportunities to train and better equip future volunteers. That effort will have to be a consistent, ongoing part of our operations to make sure our partners within local churches are prepared to meet the challenges of pursuing and welcoming a diverse population.

One final note on this subject. When it comes to volunteer training and recruiting, I want to emphasize that local church members have been our main target as we work to connect our clients with church families. However, we often get requests from area businesses, clubs and youth organizations to participate in the regular workdays for our clients. There are plenty of neighbors in Lake Travis who need assistance, so we never exclude them.

That actually provides an added bonus. Because church members always play a significant role in our efforts, the overall culture of serving through a ministry lens can rub off on the volunteers who may not be Christians. On countless occasions, we've seen God use that aspect of our work for Kingdom results.

5. Churches have to connect with people before the people connect with the churches.

For Partners in Hope and other faith-based nonprofits, we serve our isolated clients with a constant backdrop of God's love. What we do every day is a ministry. But what we *can't* do is force those clients to visit a local church, let alone join one.

We can recommend and suggest or encourage. The rest is up to them. And considering they have lived in isolation for an extended time, showing up to a big church gathering with a bunch of strangers is way out of their comfort zone. Like, in another galaxy.

To get our clients connected with churches, we started using a different tactic. Something active rather than passive.

> *Instead of pushing clients toward the church, we realized we had to pull the church toward the clients.*

It was time to reverse-engineer the process! The Lake Travis area had multiple churches with many hundreds of families, and we needed to convince them to take the lead in initiating connections.

When church members get to know our clients—volunteering at a workday, serving at a Sunday Supper, or participating in other intentional activities we use to connect—relationships can begin to develop. This intentional approach opens the door for more opportunities to connect and for friendships to bloom outside the walls of the church.

That's what flips the usual model of outreach on its head. Instead of helping people *know more about a church,* their connections allow them to *become known within the church.* The dynamic is turned upside down, in a really good way!

People who weren't initially looking for a church are motivated to attend so they can spend more time with their new, trusted friends. That process is much less overwhelming when they are greeted by someone they know at the door, and they don't have to sit by themselves during the service. They won't care how long the sermons last or whether they know the words to the songs. They'll be desperate to understand what's behind the love they recognize within the people who have served them. That experience has Kingdom potential!

The more church members these neighbors meet, the more they begin to feel like part of the family. They participate. They get involved. And when all those connections are in place, the door is wide open for those who haven't yet made a connection with the Lord.

The point is, we can't expect isolated people to connect with churches on their own.

We should pull the church toward the people rather than pushing the people to the church. Church members need to proactively reach out, drawing people in and making them feel unconditionally welcome.

Realistically, it's not an instant process. Relationships won't automatically form during one-time events, but they can grow with repeated, Christ-like contact over time. Nonprofit ministries are uniquely positioned to facilitate those connections through partnership with local churches.

6. Churches can benefit from merging the concepts of Missions and Outreach.

Somewhere along the line in church culture, people formed a distinct impression of missions as a ministry to people far away (or at least "somewhere else"). Many congregations organize mission trips to Uganda. Send missionaries to India. Collect money during missions week for orphans in Haiti. There's a sense that the people in these foreign lands have desperate needs and lead very different lives. Churches generously send resources to them, with no expectation that they would ever show up to hear a sermon.

Likewise, outreach is often framed as the church's marketing efforts to draw in people who live nearby, inviting them to participate in activities and potentially become members. That might involve running ads for a special concert. Distributing flyers with details about the Christmas Eve service. Inviting local families to a fall carnival.

The general assumption is that "neighbors" have roughly the same socio-economic profile as most of the existing congregation. These people would theoretically be a good fit and feel right at home worshipping along with others who live in the same area or share a common lifestyle.

What we discovered through our work with Partners in Hope is that missions and outreach overlap. Or at least they should. So many areas—even relatively affluent ones like Lake Travis—can have extremely diverse people with astronomical needs living right in the shadows of the church building. They are hidden in plain sight.

Perhaps these neighbors might come from a different country, speak a different language, or have a vastly different culture. Maybe they've just never been to church before. No matter how many ads they see or flyers they receive, they probably won't feel comfortable showing up at church events. They won't feel like they fit in.

> *The lesson for us has been to bring a missions mentality to local outreach.*

It should be ongoing rather than a one-time event. Relational instead of transactional. Serving someone and then sitting next to them at a worship service or a Bible study. That's very different from doing a good deed for people and never seeing them again.

If churches want to make a bigger impact for the Kingdom (and I know they do), leaders and members need to evaluate whether they are treating outreach and missions as two separate, unrelated activities. Ideally, those concepts should merge.

The best way for churches to change their cultures is to expand the view of the church. Jesus always took His disciples to people they would typically avoid. Why? Many times, the people who are hurting and in need have the most fertile hearts for God to do His work. Churches today may run the risk of missing the very people most open to God, because those neighbors don't fit the regular church profile.

As we have learned along the way, the Lord wants us to connect with hearts and souls, despite a lack of visual or social compatibility.

7. *Isolated people connect with the community through serving, not just being served.*

First things first. Partners in Hope has never had a defined requirement or expectation for its clients to "give back." We don't prescribe mandatory service hours on a generic project. Instead, through our contract, our clients agree to let us help them find ways they can engage with the community. Not a measured requirement, but a common goal.

Here's the interesting thing. Our clients often realize how the service of others has impacted their lives. They know how much progress they've made, and they are frequently eager to pay that forward by engaging with the community in some way.

Two lessons came to light in this area. First, we saw the most fulfillment in our clients when they served others in a way that fits who they are. Through our relationships, we try to help our clients identify the unique gifts and talents God has given them. Maybe they have special skills or an unusual hobby that could offer value or bring joy to someone else. Partners in Hope works to connect them with targeted opportunities for sharing their specific talents with others in the community.

A few examples might be helpful. One of our clients worked for years in the insurance industry and offered to assist other clients plagued by insurance problems. A man who was an auto mechanic helped other clients in need of car repair. A woman who loved to read developed and coordinated a book exchange program for some of the other clients who were primarily homebound. The list goes on and on. It's been exciting to identify our clients' passions and to funnel those toward helping others.

The second lesson we learned involved timing. We initially put off asking clients about serving in the community at the beginning of our relationship, thinking they just needed support first and would be ready to help other people later. But we discovered something very interesting.

> *When clients chose to share their gifts with others, they experienced a huge boost in confidence and self-esteem. It became a pivotal part of their healing process.*

As that became apparent, we had to change our approach. We began trying to connect our clients with these serving opportunities early on in our relationship—not just when they were back on their feet and already plugged in to the community.

The icing on the cake? Many times, we weren't even involved in facilitating those efforts. We hear stories weeks later about how our clients have gone above and beyond to help neighbors or friends. They know what it's like to be served, and they often gain enormous satisfaction from being on the other side of the table.

8. Understanding and managing expectations improve the impact of service.

Another lesson we learned through Partners in Hope is the strong influence of human expectations—among those who are being served, as well as those who are serving. People view the outcome of an interaction through the lens of their own expectations to determine whether it went well. Or not. And adding to the complexity, real life rarely unfolds in the way we expect.

To help illustrate that point, I want to describe some of the expectations that impact what we do at Partners in Hope.

First, consider some common expectations of *people who are serving others:*

- The people I am being asked to serve will have clear, obvious needs.
- I will be in agreement that their needs are ones that deserve to be met.
- I will feel good about helping people with this level of needs.
- The people I'm serving will react with gratitude and appreciation for the help I provide.
- The people I'm serving will use the help I offer in the way I would expect them to.

Likewise, here are some typical expectations of *people being served:*

- The people serving me will probably judge me and wonder how I ended up in this situation.
- The people serving me aren't interested in getting to know me.
- I'm supposed to stay out of the way when people are serving me.
- The people serving me shouldn't automatically assume I need assistance in every area of my life.

As you might imagine, the possibility for disappointment on both sides of a serving experience is high. Very high. Sometimes it's a positive expectation that isn't fulfilled; other times, it's a negative one that is.

> *We learned pretty quickly that helping people manage expectations was essential if we wanted serving to be a long-term, relational ministry. That requires some education and patience.*

We also learned this may be the hardest part of our job.

Leaders of churches and nonprofits need to help facilitate the understanding of expectations among everyone involved. That includes communicating why we need to adjust our expectations and what the Bible teaches us about managing those when we interact with imperfect people who are being renewed by God.

9. Flexibility and resilience are mandatory ingredients for doing the Lord's work.

As you now know, Partners in Hope has been a rapidly evolving concept from the very beginning. What started as a church mission activity became a nonprofit ministry. Helping people in need improve their living conditions morphed into ongoing relationships with the socially isolated. Teaming up with volunteers to help their neighbors transitioned into a drastically different paradigm for Kingdom building.

> *Without flexibility and resilience, we wouldn't have been able to keep pace with God's plan.*

Even today, the concept continues to transform.

As I'm putting the final touches on this book in the spring of 2020, our world is facing a global pandemic. News reports detail the horrifying death toll, crushing unemployment rates, and ever-changing guidelines for quarantine. Life as we knew it a few short months ago may never be quite the same. And God is, once again, asking us to rise to the challenge.

For Partners in Hope, we've had to quickly overhaul the way we support our clients. After all, it's tough to serve isolated people with our ongoing presence when social distancing is a health crisis requirement.

Given the circumstances, we knew the pain of isolation would become more prevalent in our community than ever before. To remain true to our mission, we responded in four ways:

First, we made a list of past and current clients in Lake Travis—more than 40 families—who we felt might be particularly susceptible to the dangers of isolation during the quarantine period. We contacted them right away and asked if we could check on them each week to see how they were doing. Only two people declined.

Next, we reached out to individual volunteers who were willing to shepherd our at-risk clients through this difficult time. Each one was assigned to a particular family. The volunteers made weekly calls to check in and pray with our clients, providing us with frequent updates about their needs and well-being.

Third, we promoted four groups of volunteer opportunities to our partners within the community: meal delivery, errand running, yard work and simple home repairs. We asked volunteers to sign up and be available to respond as we learned of specific needs to be met among our clients.

Finally, despite being physically off the grid during the pandemic, we let our ministry partners know we were still available to help. We encouraged them to contact us if they learned of people in the community who were suffering from isolation. While we had to temporarily suspend our normal, group-based serving activities, we used this opportunity to get creative in helping those in need. We began connecting with different people, working with some new volunteers, applying more technology solutions, and serving in ways we might never have otherwise explored.

It's been a wild ride, but we're making it work. And the truth is, I'm quite certain this won't be the last time God asks us to pivot and change our direction. We have learned the importance of flexibility and resilience in serving the Lord and serving others.

That's one lesson we need to remember every day.

CHAPTER SEVEN

THE APPLICATION

*I got to watch God work while I was eating
a Whataburger. Cheese, no onions.*

One of the strongest ways to illustrate the impact of applying all these lessons we've learned is through an example. Well, actually two. It's another unexpected connection that God used in miraculous ways.

Highlighting the Example

Our contact at the Lake Travis Crisis Ministries reached out to Partners in Hope to tell us about a man named Scott who really needed our help. He was in his 60s and had lived in the Austin area for most of his life. His ongoing battle with depression and addiction had dragged him down to a dark place.

When I first met Scott through a meeting arranged at the Crisis Ministries, his depression was palpable. Disheveled appearance. Shoulders hunched. Head down, eyes fixed on the floor. Everything about his demeanor screamed total defeat, shame and embarrassment. It was heartbreaking.

He told me the past few years had been almost unbearable—a bitter divorce, dwindling income, plummeting self-esteem. Although his daughter had been living with him, they became estranged and she moved out. When the only person left in his life disappeared, he fell into a downward spiral of isolation and bad decisions. The house he'd owned for years was falling apart, and his neighbors weren't shy about expressing their displeasure at his lack of care.

Scott felt like the walls were crashing in on him, and he numbed the pain with drugs and alcohol.

I then asked Scott to tell me a little bit about his life before all of this happened. Without hesitation, he told me that his greatest passion was music. At that moment, I thought I detected the tiniest hint of a smile. He said he'd been a rocker in the Austin music scene for 40 years and loved performing with his band, night after night. He also played a number of different musical instruments, although he was forced to sell most of those to pawn shops years ago.

As we continued our conversation, I discovered that Scott had actually grown up in the church. Unfortunately, somewhere along the way, people there had made him feel judged and unworthy. Those negative encounters left him with some painful scars.

I wondered how Scott would react to our contract agreement, given that background, but thankfully he was willing to make the commitment. He was ready for someone to walk alongside him in the journey to find the brighter side of life.

Partners in Hope planned a workday at Scott's house, and we recruited volunteers from a nearby church to make some much-needed improvements around his property. These guys had a heart for people like Scott, and I knew they would be great ambassadors for the church.

An occasional glimmer of hope crossed Scott's face during the construction process, and I could tell something inside him was changing. Although Scott's insecurity made him reluctant to venture out, we finally convinced him to join one of our Sunday Suppers at a local church near his house.

Some of the guys who had volunteered to work on his property were attending the dinner that night, and they invited Scott to join them at the table.

I think it's important to highlight the meaning behind that action. With Partners in Hope, we approach all of our clients with a spirit of equality.

We never, ever want people to feel "less than" because of their situations, nor to position ourselves as the heroes who are doing them a favor.

We are all children of God, and our clients are worthy friends and neighbors. The Sunday Suppers provide us with great opportunities to demonstrate that principle.

As Scott sat down with the other men, any illusion of separation was shattered. They shared one table. It was five, equally valued peers enjoying a meal together and engaging in some great discussions. For the first time, I started to see Scott being drawn into conversation. Even chiming in with the group.

These men kept in touch with Scott after that night and continued to build the relationship. They eventually invited him to come to their Men's Bible Study on Tuesday nights, and he agreed. Scott learned from these men and, likewise, they learned from him. It was a life-changing decision for all of them.

While that's certainly a positive outcome, the story doesn't end there. It gets better.

Continuing the Story

Five months later, Partners in Hope got another referral from Lake Travis Crisis Ministries to a man named Max. He'd grown up in the Hudson Bend area and raised his family there. Now he was divorced with children living across the country. He had been a painter for years—until he fell and suffered a spinal cord injury. He typically used a cane to get around, and he was experiencing severe pain. Then, in a terrible twist of fate, Max's faithful dog of 14 years passed away. His only companion was gone.

Max was inconsolable, and the addiction to pain killers quickly followed.

When I met Max, he was doing his best to stay upbeat about the future. He agreed to partner with us, and we organized a great workday at his property. As I got to know Max better, I discovered that he was also a former Austin rocker who loved guitars and music. I immediately told him he needed to meet my friend Scott, and I couldn't wait to introduce them.

After trying several times to get Scott and Max to show up to the same Sunday Supper event, I decided to take matters into my own hands. One morning, I called Max and asked if we could meet at his house for lunch. I would bring the Whataburgers and, with a little luck, Scott.

Max was immediately on board. The call with Scott wasn't quite as well received, since he was still fairly uncomfortable about socializing with new people. I had no idea if he would show up, but I gave him the address and told him I had a cheeseburger waiting for him.

Fifteen minutes later, Scott arrived at Max's door. After the some-what-awkward introductions, Max started to show Scott a few of his guitars.

> *For the next hour, I basically sat in silence while a friendship emerged and the two of them reminisced about their rock-and-roll days.*

They actually knew some of the same people, and they each shared lively stories about performing on Sixth Street in downtown Austin. These guys totally hit it off.

Several months later, after Scott and Max had really gotten to know each other at some of our fellowship events, I asked them if they might be interested in performing at one of our Sunday Suppers. Neither one had played a "real gig" in ten years and, of course, they'd never performed together. For them, this idea was equal parts exhilarating *and* terrifying.

Max jumped at the opportunity right away though, ready to practice and develop a set list. Scott approached it with more of a let's-wing-it attitude. They did manage to have a couple rehearsals and gathered together some sound equipment. Later that summer, we held our Sunday Supper event in the park, with Max and Scott providing our live entertainment.

Despite some early nerves, they quickly relaxed into their swaggering rocker grooves as the attendees cheered and danced. It was an amazing sight, especially considering how far they'd both come. After the last notes were played, the audience rewarded them with an enthusiastic standing ovation.

> *I watched in awe as these two men—once devastated by isolation—shared heartwarming hugs and joyful smiles.*

Leading up to their big performance, Scott had begun attending church with his friends from the Men's Bible Study group. He invited Max to join him, and they both became regular attendees. In addition, Scott started playing keyboard with the church worship team on Sunday mornings, and Max became a frequent participant at the Wednesday night services and dinners.

The moral of the story?

> *God used connections to save these men from the pain of isolation, and our Kingdom partnership created an environment for that to happen.*

Working together—as nonprofits and a local church—we were pulling people out of isolation and walking them toward the Kingdom of God. That was such an inspiration to see!

Keeping it Real

Now for a reality check. Since life is messy and doesn't deliver the fairy-tale endings of Disney movies, I do feel compelled to add this important footnote.

A year later, Max had a terrible fall and moved to live with his daughter on the east coast. He calls me frequently (sometimes once a week) to tell me how much he misses fellowship with his Lake Travis friends. On the upside, he is surrounded by family. He is well cared for, and he feels loved and respected.

As for Scott, his life since the big performance hasn't been all rainbows and butterflies either. He still struggles occasionally with some depression. But here's the difference. He has a church family—a community of people to love him through the hard times and encourage him to walk through difficulty in a more healthy way. He remains committed to worshipping and serving at his church every chance he gets.

I remember getting a phone call from Scott one day, completely out of the blue. His voice cracked as he spoke, and I could tell he was almost crying. But I discovered it was a "good cry"—with tears of joy and appreciation. He thanked me in the most sincere way for walking down the road with him over the years and helping him get connected to his church. It meant the world to him.

That was an indelible moment, and I prayed right then: "God, I don't know why I get the privilege of doing this, but thank you."

Integrating the Lessons

Before we finish this chapter, I hope you'll take a moment to really think about the remarkable outcomes for these two men. Where they started. Where they ended up. How their journeys were influenced by unexpected connections.

It took years for Partners in Hope to learn the lessons that contributed to their success.

> *Examples like this show God's infinite goodness*
> *when we are patient and work to apply*
> *the knowledge we've gained.*

- We recognized that Scott and Max were both suffering from social isolation (not just homes in disrepair) because they had chronic issues and no support systems.
- Serving these men became a long-term, collaborative effort between Lake Travis Crisis Ministries, Partners in Hope, and a local church.
- The church leaders set the example for blending the concepts of missions and outreach, embracing neighbors with diverse lifestyles and backgrounds.
- The church volunteers had some training and experience in building relationships that would benefit the Kingdom.
- The church volunteers managed their expectations, and they were proactive about making the connections.
- Scott and Max found great joy and confidence through sharing their musical talents, demonstrating they had value to offer others.
- Scott and Max were able to integrate into a church family because people really cared for them and were willing to walk with them throughout their journeys.

Lessons learned, lessons applied. Amen!

CHAPTER EIGHT

THE OPPORTUNITY

*Whether you want the whole recipe or you're just curious about
a key ingredient, I've got some food for thought.*

This is the point in the book where *our* story can become *your* opportunity.

Whether you are involved with a church ministry or a faith-based nonprofit, the lessons we learned with Partners in Hope could provide the motivation you need to begin rewiring your Kingdom Serving Paradigm.

My prayer is that everything we've invested into our ministry can continue to bear fruit in other areas and in other ways. God always goes far beyond anything we could ever think or imagine, so I'm excited to see how these principles translate into His plan.

Some people will simply take the insights and inspirations they gathered from our stories into their neighborhoods as they serve those in need. Others may feel compelled to carefully emulate our connection-based process. Either way, this chapter will provide you with a framework for moving forward. You'll also find helpful tools in the back of the book in our Resource Guide, as well as on our website at UnexpectedConnections.org.

So how do you want to get started?

Is God calling you to rewire your community to fight social isolation and to grow the Kingdom?

If you take that challenge, you may be a pioneer for promoting this approach in your community. In some neighborhoods, the silo effect that separates many churches and nonprofits may be fairly robust. In others, these groups might actually tend to "compete" for the opportunity to champion certain causes. That's not uncommon—and it explains why change can be hard. But it's not impossible.

Here are some steps we hope can help make it easier to join forces with other faith-based organizations in your area.

1. Reiterate the Common Goal

Start by communicating your shared goal: to build the Kingdom. Churches and nonprofits are on the same team! If you can use that truth to set the tone for conversations about change in your community, you'll be ahead of the game. That's what makes these partnerships really count.

Now a dose of reality. When you talk about building the Kingdom together, everyone will probably give you an enthusiastic YES! However, the road to get there often looks different for every organization. Many groups, ironically, view Kingdom goals as something to be accomplished separately. Church goals aren't the same as nonprofit goals—or at least that seems to be the standard perception.

This will be your opportunity to change that.

When nonprofits keep the Kingdom mindset front and center, they'll be driven to do more than serve people in need. They'll want to see these neighbors connect to a local church family and come into the body of Christ.

For churches, the Kingdom mindset leads them to think of nonprofit ministries as partners who can help equip their members to reach a certain segment of the community, drawing them into church families and connecting them with God.

Different starting point, same destination.

> *Approach your discussions with potential partners as opportunities to align your goals and accelerate your progress.*

Working together means you can better address the needs of the people in your community. You can be better stewards of resources rather than duplicating efforts. And you can collectively do a better job at bringing more neighbors into the body of Christ.

You have to admit, those are some really strong incentives to start breaking down the silos and create a new type of synergy. At the same time, patience will be an important virtue. Rewiring the Kingdom Serving Paradigm in your community is much less of a bulldozer production and more of a chisel operation. While Kingdom partnership requires perseverance, it's certainly worthy of the effort.

2. Communicate the Paradigm Shift

Within the context of sharing a common Kingdom goal, you'll want to boldly describe the paradigm for this new community partnership. That's a critical step, since you're basically suggesting a complete overhaul to the usual work process between nonprofits and churches.

Old Way of Working	New Way of Working
Separate Silos	Collaborative Partnerships
Project-Based	Relationship-Based
Short-Term	Long-Term
Generic Plans	Customized Plans

Leaders of churches and nonprofit ministries are usually all in favor of cooperation for serving neighbors in need. Their attitudes and intent are positive. The problem? Cooperation isn't enough to get the Kingdom results we all want. That requires a different vision—one that involves *collaboration*.

We know a thing or two about the challenges of trying to explain this critical distinction.

Enthusiastically talking to your potential community partners about collaboration, common goals and rewiring the paradigm will likely elicit some vague smiles and tentative head nodding.

> *The best way to really break through the comprehension barrier is to actually show them what that change would look like.*

Let them see the limitations of the current process. The potential of the new paradigm. The expanded opportunities for the Kingdom.

I am very much a visual person, and I have drawn many a picture on a napkin. Creating these diagrams has helped me to see and communicate the differences, so I hope they will help you as well.

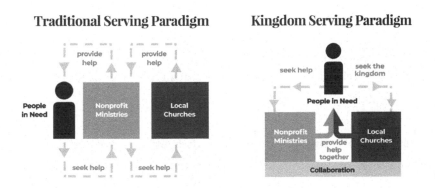

You'll find these full-size visuals in the Resource Guide at the back of the book, or you can download them from our website at UnexpectedConnections.org.

The commonality for both versions is that nonprofit ministries still have a unique doorway to connect to people in need. That remains a constant.

The specific ministry focus for each of these nonprofits—addiction, divorce, adoption, hunger—provides an access point into the lives of people who could be connected to the body of Christ. Meeting their needs is not the end goal but rather a means of ministry.

With the Kingdom Serving Paradigm, the silos are eliminated. Everything that happens after the initial contact is driven by a Kingdom partnership. Nonprofits strategically reach out to join forces with area churches to serve their common neighbors in need. The nonprofits are also instrumental in equipping and mobilizing church members for ministry.

Through these sustained relationships, this collaborative effort can have a much greater impact on the physical, emotional and spiritual needs of those being served.

Best of all, this partnership creates and extends an on-ramp for the church to receive new families and move them more deliberately toward the Kingdom.

When you feel like you're fighting the underlying current of the we-don't-usually-work-that-way mindset, I hope you can use these images to help demonstrate the incredible paradigm for collaborating to achieve a common goal.

3. Describe the Benefits

Rewiring the way ministry programs in your community combine to serve people involves some ongoing conversations. After you've highlighted the shared goals and provided graphic support to explain the paradigm, you're ready to take the next step.

To get buy-in from other groups in the community, you'll need to be able to articulate why these partnerships matter and what specific advantages they will produce. In other words, be ready to respond when they're thinking, "what's in it for me?"

No, that's not a selfish attitude. Not at all. It's just how people naturally process information and determine their level of motivation to make the changes you're proposing. If you want to be successful in forming these partnerships, you'll need to think and speak from that perspective.

Here's something to keep in mind. Some people may, unfortunately, perceive the shared goal of bringing neighbors into the Kingdom as idealistic or even cliché. They might need some additional encouragement. In other words, you want to spell it out.

> *Give your potential new partners clearly defined reasons why they should want to help you tear down the silos.*

To do that, share some of the operational benefits that can be gained by working in unison as the body of Christ.

For Nonprofits

In the Kingdom Serving Paradigm, nonprofits have strong incentives to team up more closely with local churches.

These partnerships increase the likelihood that church members will become genuinely excited about a nonprofit's mission and purpose, prompting them to volunteer on a regular basis. And when nonprofits have a more consistent flow of volunteers, they can step up to make bigger commitments than they would on their own. That also creates a path for nonprofits to provide frequent volunteers with specialized training—something they probably wouldn't do for people volunteering on a one-time basis.

As an example, Partners in Hope was able to add new client families every month only because of the multiple, ongoing church partnerships we established. That, in turn, led to more serving opportunities. Which paved the way for more volunteers returning month after month. Which allowed us to better educate and empower all of those who were making connections in the community on behalf of Partners in Hope.

By extending their church relationships and engaging repetitive volunteers, nonprofit ministries can become more productive and impactful in serving the community. Even better, these partnerships increase the odds that churches will commit to providing greater resources and long-term financial support.

For Churches

The Kingdom Serving Paradigm moves church volunteers closer to the front lines for supporting people in need. This typically increases the emotional connection between church members and their mission activities. The more they understand the circumstances and challenges of isolated people (or other demographics being served), the more they feel compelled to get involved on a deeper level. As these volunteers develop a greater passion for serving others, they can become strong disciples who are adept at sharing the love of Jesus with people from all walks of life, even those in their own neighborhoods.

Besides building a stronger sense of community, the church/nonprofit partnership can help to raise the visibility of churches in their individual neighborhoods.

Over time, that elevated awareness has the potential to translate into more interest in the church, increased church membership, greater resources and additional volunteers to participate in mission work.

As church members mature, they will recognize the benefits of Kingdom partnership across a broader community. Where they once might have sought out a new church because they felt pigeonholed by their own congregation's typical "avenues" of serving, the Kingdom mindset removes all the limitations. They can tap into a wide range of meaningful serving opportunities with any of the community's faith-based organizations, while remaining part of their own church families.

All of these partnership advantages can add tremendous value for local churches and nonprofits. But, without a doubt, there's also a cost involved with this approach. No partnership exists without making some sacrifices, giving up some control, investing outside your organization, and sharing leadership duties.

There's also the realization that results take time. Delayed gratification is the rule, not the exception. Seeds have to be planted and fields tended before the harvest. But just remember this: Your willingness to accept these Kingdom costs can lead to a wealth of Kingdom benefits.

4. Provide Some Targeted Strategies

For Nonprofits

To help nonprofit ministries move forward to partner more closely with local churches, the following strategies may be helpful:

- **Initiate relationships with hyper-local churches** through ongoing contact with ministry leaders (not just senior pastors but leaders at every level). Unless you already have an established relationship with the senior pastor, you may find those connections are harder to make. Start by building relationships with other ministry leaders.
- **Commit to a long-term investment** of time and energy to build and strengthen those relationships. Your initial attempts to connect may go nowhere, and the process will be slow. But the one who keeps knocking will eventually get their attention.

- **Increase your visibility by participating in church activities.** Attend their worship services, and make the effort to meet some of their leaders. If they offer community events open to the public, show up and introduce yourself to some of the members. Just remember that the goal of your networking is not to gain support for your nonprofit, but to look for partnership doorways.
- **Regularly attend gatherings of local pastors and ministry leaders in your area.** Work to build relationships and demonstrate your desire to be part of the ministerial community.
- **Participate in fellowship events** sponsored by churches or other faith-based groups to help make more connections and build relationships.
- **Facilitate service opportunities** that deliberately "cross pollenate" efforts among multiple nonprofits and churches to deliver greater impact.

As nonprofit organizations start to make progress in building these relationships, they may find it valuable to document the resources available to them through the ministry groups of different churches. Having a clear picture of the options will allow them to select potential partners for each serving opportunity that will best meet a client's needs.

Here's an example for nonprofits:

Resource Inventory Tool
for Nonprofit Ministries

Potential Church Partners	Ministry Areas	Ministry Contacts	
Grace Lutheran Church	Adults	Bob Smith	(555) 123-4567
	Missions	Judy Garza	(555) 123-9876
	Youth	Don Reed	(555) 123-3579
Highland Presbyterian Church	Women	Angie Martin	(555) 123-1357
	Outreach	Emilio Diaz	(555) 123-7351
	Special Needs	Linda Gibbs	(555) 123-8604

For Churches

Local churches interested in teaming up with faith-based nonprofits in their area can follow these strategies to help fuel the partnership:

- **Work to change the perception of nonprofit ministries** to be discipling partners (rather than competitors), working toward the same goal.
- **Identify nonprofits that will help to equip your members for discipleship** and invite them to do training sessions in your church.

- **Educate your congregation and leadership about the purpose of these nonprofits.** What segments of the community do they reach? How could your church better minister to those segments in partnership with the nonprofit? Highlight how their missions align with yours, and describe how you would like to strategically partner with them.

- **Ask church members to provide their feedback** and suggestions for collaboration with your potential nonprofit ministry partners.

- **Publicize opportunities for church members** to give of their time, talent, and treasure on behalf of the nonprofit ministries you see as potential partners.

- **Facilitate participation in events and efforts** that integrate with the church's existing missions and studies.

- **Commit to a long-term investment** with nonprofit ministry partners in terms of funding and volunteers, allowing them to operate at a more sustained level. Begin with a small, ongoing amount, and let the nonprofit know you will revisit the partnership annually to evaluate progress on your common goals.

- **Generously lend expertise to ministry partners** to help spur growth and expansion, which are critical since these nonprofits are still the doorway to people in need. Nonprofits often lack administrative expertise, so they can greatly benefit from church members and staff with specific skills to help their organizations.

- **Search for alternative ways to support nonprofits** other than cash and volunteers. One of our church partners told us they wanted to support Partners in Hope, but didn't have cash they could allocate. Instead, they offered us some available space at their facility that we now use for an office.

Following the same line of thinking, churches can also benefit from documenting the resources available to them through nonprofit ministries or other congregations in their community. Here's an example:

Resource Inventory Tool
for Churches

Potential Partners: Nonprofits or Churches	Ministry Areas	Ministry Contacts	
Main Street Homeless Shelter	Temporary housing; counseling	John Dodge	(555) 123-8642
Bread of Life Food Bank	Canned food and staples; some household supplies	Carla Cantu	(555) 123-6068
Workforce Ministries of West King County	Resumé development, mock interviews, support group, job leads	Malik Azami	(555) 123-3456
First Baptist Church	Addiction recovery services and support	Stewart Long	(555) 123-0204
St. John Episcopal Church	ESL program	Maria Fuentes	(555) 123-3951

5. Create a Customized Plan

Every person you serve is different, so the formula for successfully serving them can't be the same every time.

When an isolated person reaches out to a nonprofit for help, that organization can immediately team up with other faith-based groups in the community to determine a customized solution.

> *The most important thing is to keep the clients' unique challenges as the focal point of the process.*

Then draw from the inventory of resources available to each of your collaborative team members and determine the best possible way to meet specific needs.

For instance, if a client mentions having a particular religious affiliation, you might enlist volunteers from a local church of that denomination to help with home improvement. Otherwise, you might call for support from the church closest to the person's neighborhood. If the client family has teenagers, look for a church with an active youth ministry. The same goes for single moms, recovering addicts or abuse victims. Identify the clients' needs, and find a church best positioned to meet them.

Using a Partnership Mapping Tool can help to clearly document the process.

Here's an example:

Partnership Mapping Tool
Kingdom Serving Opportunities

Person/Family to be Served	Specific Needs	Best Partner to Engage for Meeting Those Needs
Erik & Kylie Anderson Two boys (ages 1 and 3)	Home repair	Highland Presbyterian Church
	Food support	Bread of Life Food Bank
	Unemployment assistance	Workforce Ministries of West King County
Connie Rodriquez	Home repair	Grace Lutheran Church
	Diabetes care support	Methodist Healthcare Ministries Community Nurse
	Crisis counseling	Arise Mental Health Ministries
Shawn Washington	Temporary housing	Main Street Homeless Shelter
	Special needs support	Highland Presbyterian Church
	Addiction assistance	First Baptist Recovery Services

This tool can be shared among nonprofits and churches to establish a customized team dedicated to serving an isolated person or family. It can provide much-needed transparency for everyone involved, and it can easily be updated as new needs emerge and additional partners are required.

You'll find copies of the Partnership Mapping Tool and the Resource Inventory Sheets in the Resource Guide section at the back of the book. Or you can visit our website at UnexpectedConnections.org to download full-size versions in pdf format.

6. Commit to Ongoing Collaboration

Last but not least, be realistic about the length of time it will take to implement this new paradigm in a smooth, seamless fashion.

Some people in leadership positions for churches and nonprofits may be naturally wired to resist change, even when a fresh approach offers great promise. That's just human nature. You'll be trying to tear down the silos, and they'll be rebuilding them at the same pace. Be patient. Deep breathing probably wouldn't hurt either.

In my experience as a nonprofit leader, I learned the importance of keeping a presence with the church, no matter how insignificant it might seem. You never know when a change in staff members or circumstances could suddenly open a new door.

And if you end up working with partners who simply aren't quite as committed to the relationship as you are, don't let that stop you. Just dive in and do your best to educate them about the outcomes you can achieve by working together.

Keep looking through the lens of the people who need to be part of the Kingdom and concentrate on how your partnership could help them connect. Instead of telling potential partners all about your church or ministry, focus on the needs of the client. Describe how those partners could be instrumental in guiding a client to the body of Christ through a team effort.

There's no way around it. These partnerships will require an ongoing investment of time and energy. But always remember that the precious return on that investment will benefit the Kingdom of God.

If you are interested in starting a nonprofit ministry
like Partners in Hope and would like more information,
please send me a message at:
PartnersInHopeLakeTravis@gmail.com

CONCLUSION

---&---

"Faith is taking the first step even when
you can't see the whole staircase."

—Martin Luther King, Jr.

For much of our journey with Partners in Hope, not being able to see the top of the staircase was the least of our challenges. We frequently couldn't see the *next step*. But God kept giving us lessons in faith, with just enough encouragement to push forward.

Piece by piece, God revealed more of His plan to us. He'd show us just enough glimpses of His work to let us know we were heading in the right direction. Knowing that I am a "processor," God also allowed us to move at a slow enough pace to prevent me from getting overwhelmed or lost in the puzzle.

He showed us the urgency of supporting people who've been devastated by social isolation. He led us to make connections and build lasting relationships in ways we never anticipated—with our clients, with churches, and with other nonprofit ministries in the community. And then He made the most startling revelation of all.

Our job at Partners in Hope wasn't to find solutions for our
clients. It was to help the church become the solution.

Our purpose was to equip more volunteers as part of discipleship. To connect the body of Christ with a greater number of people in the community. To shepherd more neighbors into church families and lead them to become part of the Kingdom.

We never could have imagined that our mission to serve people in need would change so drastically. To our amazement, we watched God rewire the standard serving paradigm and establish Kingdom partnerships that bonded a community in the most powerful ways. It was something we never could have accomplished or even envisioned on our own.

Day after day, we remain in complete awe of God's unexpected connections. In fact, this book is yet another example.

I shared with you in the Introduction that leading a nonprofit ministry was never on my career radar. Neither was writing a book. But through the words you've read in each of these chapters, I've had the honor of making an unexpected connection with you. I'm grateful for that, and I want to thank you for spending the time to learn more about our ministry.

One of the most gratifying parts of this whole experience has been discovering the ripple effect of blessings that God has allowed to flow from the relationships we've formed. I hope and pray that you will also become part of this cascade of impact.

If your organization implements some or all of the principles in this book, I'd love to hear about your experiences. Please take a moment to send me an email at PartnersInHopeLakeTravis@gmail.com. We might even post an excerpt from your story on our website (with your permission, of course) to let others see how the ripple effect from this unique ministry framework continues to amplify the impact for the body of Christ.

Once again, it all comes back to this:

We can do the most good for the Kingdom of God if all parts of the Kingdom work together.

May all of your connections be blessed,

Matt

RESOURCE GUIDE

❖

Reference Materials

The following list includes books and articles about the impact of social isolation that may provide support for your community's efforts to fight this epidemic.

Bowling Alone: The Collapse and Revival of American Community by Robert D. Putnam (Simon Schuster: August 7, 2001). https://www.amazon.com/Bowling-Alone-Collapse-American-Community/dp/B01N94FW0P/ref=sr_1_2?dchild=1&keywords=Bowling+Alone&qid=1585919528&s=books&sr=1-2

"How Social Isolation is Killing Us" by Dr. Dhruv Khullar (*New York Times*: December 22, 2016). https://www.nytimes.com/2016/12/22/upshot/how-social-isolation-is-killing-us.html

"Isolation Nation" by Allison Abrams (*Psychology Today*: January 15, 2019). https://www.psychologytoday.com/us/blog/nurturing-self-compassion/201901/isolation-nation

"Loneliness and Social Isolation as Risk Factors for Mortality" by Julianne Holt-Lunstad, Timothy B. Smith, Mark Baker, Tyler Harris and David Stephenson (Journal for the Association of Psychological Science: March 11, 2015). https://journals.sagepub.com/doi/10.1177/1745691614568352

"The Loneliness Epidemic" (Health Resources & Services Administration: January 2019). https://www.hrsa.gov/enews/past-issues/2019/january-17/loneliness-epidemic

Loneliness: Human Nature and the Need for Social Connection by John T. Cacioppo and William Patrick (W.W. Norton & Company: August 10, 2009). https://www.amazon.com/Loneliness-Human-Nature-Social-Connection/dp/0393335283

"Loneliness is Harmful to our Nation's Health" by Claire Pomeroy (*Scientific American*: March 20, 2019). https://blogs.scientificamerican.com/observations/loneliness-is-harmful-to-our-nations-health/

The Lonely American: Drifting Apart in the Twenty-First Century by Jacqueline Olds, M.D., and Richard S. Schwartz, M.D. (Beacon Press: February 1, 2010). https://www.amazon.com/Lonely-American-Drifting-Twenty-first-Century/dp/0807000353

"Millennials and the Loneliness Epidemic" by Neil Howe (*Forbes*: May 3, 2019). https://www.forbes.com/sites/neilhowe/2019/05/03/millennials-and-the-loneliness-epidemic/#14ea2f087676

"New Study Reveals Loneliness at Epidemic Levels in America" by Ellie Polack (Cigna Global Health Services: May 1, 2018). https://www.cigna.com/newsroom/news-releases/2018/new-cigna-study-reveals-loneliness-at-epidemic-levels-in-america

Partners in Hope website (2020). https://www.PartnersInHopeLakeTravis.org

"Social Isolation and Loneliness are America's Next Public Health Issues" by Jay Bhatt, DO, and Jonathan McKinney, MPH (Becker's Hospital Review: December 2, 2019). https://www.beckershospitalreview.com/population-health/social-isolation-and-loneliness-are-america-s-next-public-health-issue.html

"Social Isolation in America" by Paola Parigi and Warner Henson II (Stanford University Annual Review of Sociology: July 2014). https://sociology.stanford.edu/publications/social-isolation-america

"Social Isolation: It Could Kill You" by Amy Novotney (Journal of the American Psychological Association: May 2019). https://www.apa.org/monitor/2019/05/ce-corner-isolation

"Social Isolation, Loneliness in Older People Pose Health Risks" (National Institute on Aging: April 23, 2019). https://www.nia.nih.gov/news/social-isolation-loneliness-older-people-pose-health-risks

"20 Facts About Senior Isolation That Will Stun You" by Sarah Stevenson (A Place for Mom/Senior Living Blog: November 15, 2019). https://www.aplaceformom.com/blog/10-17-14-facts-about-senior-isolation/

Available for download at www.UnexpectedConnections.org

The Serving Model
Partners in Hope

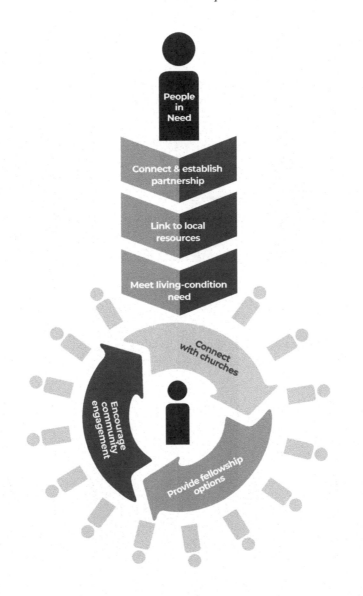

Available for download at www.UnexpectedConnections.org

Traditional Serving Paradigm
Silos and Separation

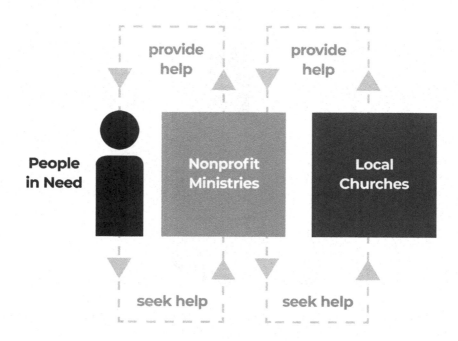

People in Need

provide help

Nonprofit Ministries

provide help

Local Churches

seek help

seek help

Kingdom Serving Paradigm
Collaboration and Communication

Available for download at www.UnexpectedConnections.org

The Ripple Effect
How the Serving Process Impacts the Community

The Problem: Isolation

Flow:
From stagnant water of isolation to living water of loving community

Ripples:
Indications of flow downstream where relationships develop outside of planned activities

Intentional Actions Create Flow:

- Home Improvement
- Small Groups
- Sunday Suppers
- Meal Delivery
- Volunteer Equipping
- Ongoing Response to Needs

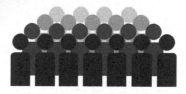

The Vision:
A community empowered to work together to eliminate hopelessness and isolation

Available for download at www.UnexpectedConnections.org

Resource Inventory Tool
for Nonprofit Ministries

Potential Church Partners	Ministry Areas	Ministry Contacts

Available for download at www.UnexpectedConnections.org

Resource Inventory Tool
for Churches

Potential Partners: Nonprofits or Churches	Services Provided	Contact Person

Available for download at www.UnexpectedConnections.org

Partnership Mapping Tool
Kingdom Serving Opportunities

Person/Family to be Served	Specific Needs	Best Partner to Engage for Meeting Those Needs

Available for download at www.UnexpectedConnections.org

ABOUT MATT PEACOCK

Matt Peacock is the Founder of Partners in Hope—Lake Travis and has been the Executive Director since 2014. Prior to that time, he was the Lead Pastor for the Church at Bee Cave (Austin, TX). His previous roles include Discipleship and Missions Pastor with the Church at Canyon Creek (Austin, TX), Discipleship Pastor with Mountain View Baptist Church (Tucson, AZ), Youth and Administration Pastor with University Baptist Church (San Antonio, TX), and Youth Pastor with Bee Cave Baptist Church (Austin, TX).

In addition to serving with these congregations, Matt has been a leadership instructor with Concordia University and a workshop leader for conferences sponsored by the Texas Christian Community Development Network (TXCCDN). Throughout his ministry career that started in 1994, Matt's pastoral duties have included preaching, teaching, counseling, mentoring, missions and outreach activities, discipleship, leader/team development, community collaboration, strategic planning, financial administration, and staff/volunteer oversight.

Matt earned a Master of Arts degree in Christian Education from Southwestern Baptist Theological Seminary (Fort Worth, TX) and a Master of Public Administration degree from Texas State University (San Marcos, TX). He also holds a Bachelor of Arts degree in Political Science from the University of Oklahoma (Norman, OK).

Matt and his wife Cynthia have two grown children, Nathan and Kennan, as well as an 80-pound German Shepherd who fully believes she is a lap dog.

Email: PartnersInHopeLakeTravis@gmail.com
Phone: (512) 751-5877

in **Connect with Matt on LinkedIn:** Matt Peacock
𝕐 **Follow Matt on Twitter:** @MattPeacock15

ABOUT PARTNERS IN HOPE

———— ✦ ————

Partners in Hope—Lake Travis is an Austin, Texas-based nonprofit ministry that applies a unique approach to serve people who are suffering from social isolation in nearby Lake Travis. Founded in 2011, the organization strategically collaborates with other faith-based groups throughout the community to help meet the physical, emotional and spiritual needs of disconnected neighbors. Working together, these ministry partnerships are making a powerful impact for the Kingdom of God.

Connection Guided Partners in Hope connects people with the targeted resources and support they need to escape the hopelessness of isolation and begin integrating into a loving community.

Relationship Focused Partners in Hope develops compassionate, ongoing relationships with clients and commits to walk with them through a difficult season of life rather than providing a one-time crisis response.

Collaboration Powered Partners in Hope operates in collaboration with other nonprofit ministries and churches, helping equip volunteers and members to effectively pursue isolated people and draw them into local church families.

Kingdom Driven Partners in Hope empowers the Kingdom of God within the community to join forces in an unconventionally beautiful way to help build the body of Christ.

If we can serve you in any way, please contact us at
PartnersInHopeLakeTravis@gmail.com.

CONNECT

Matt Peacock
Executive Director
Partners in Hope—Lake Travis

www.PartnersInHopeLakeTravis.org
www.Unexpected Connections.org

Email: PartnersInHopeLakeTravis@gmail.com
Phone: (512) 751-5877
Address: 15104 N. Flamingo Drive, Austin, Texas 78734

f   **Follow us on Facebook:** Partners in Hope Lake Travis
in   **Connect with Matt on LinkedIn:** Matt Peacock
𝕐   **Follow Matt on Twitter:** @MattPeacock15

To support our work with a one-time or recurring donation, please visit: PartnersInHopeLakeTravis.org/donate/

If you are interested in starting a nonprofit ministry like Partners in Hope and would like more information, please send a message to PartnersInHopeLakeTravis@gmail.com.

Partners in Hope—Lake Travis is a tax-exempt 501(c)3 organization.